TCHAIKOVSKY

his life and times

Wilson Strutte

Paganiniana Publications, Inc.
211 West Sylvania Avenue, Neptune City, N.J. 07753

To my mother and father and Katie, my sister

ISBN 0-87666-641-1

Tchaikovsky: His Life and Times by Wilson Strutte was originally published in 1979 by Midas Books, 12 Dene Way, Speldhurst, Tunbridge Wells, Kent TN3 0NX England. Copyright ©1979 by Wilson Strutte, reprinted by permission of the publisher.

Expanded Edition of *Tchaikovsky: His Life and Times* ©1981 by Paganiniana Publications, Inc. A considerable amount of new material has been added to the original text, including but not limited to illustrations and their captions. Copyright is claimed for this new material.

Published by PAGANINIANA PUBLICATIONS, INC.
211 West Sylvania Avenue
Neptune City, New Jersey 07753

Acknowledgements

I must thank Trevelian Bareham, Kate Aldridge, June Hall and my family for their support, enthusiasm and patience. Also I would like to mention the late Ben Smith who was a constant source of encouragement. Most important of all I must thank Marjorie Bidmead, without whose help this book would not have been written. To her, my deepest gratitude.

Illustrations on pages 7, 8, 19, 20, 25 (lower), 35, 39, 41, 42, 51, 55, 71, 74, 77, 81, 85, 92, 97 (upper), 100, 102, 103, 104, 109 (lower), 110 (upper), 111, 112, 125, 126, 127, 128, 130, 139 and 140 were supplied by, and reproduced with the kind permission of, The Mary Evans Picture Library, London.

The frontispiece and illustrations on pages 3, 5, 10, 12, 13 (upper), 14, 16, 18, 21 (upper), 26, 33, 50 (upper), 56, 58, 75, 79, 94, 116, 119, 131, 132, 133, 134, 135, 138 (upper), 144 and 148 were supplied by, and reproduced with the kind permission of, The Novosti Press Agency, Moscow.

Selected Bibliography

Abraham, Gerald — Tchaikovsky: A Short Biography. London, 1944 — ed. Tchaikovsky: A Symposium. London, 1945

Bowen, Catherine Drinker and von Meck, Barbara — Beloved Friend, New York, 1937

Evans, Edwin — Tchaikovsky. London, 1906 (Master Musicians Series: revised edition, 1935)

Garden, Edward — Tchaikovsky. (Master Musicians Series) London, 1973

Hoffman, Michel — Tchaikovsky. London, 1962

Pipes, Richard — Russia Under The Old Regime. London, 1974

Tchaikovsky, Modest — The Life and Letters of Peter Illych Tchaikovsky (abr. Eng. trans. by Rosa Newmarch). London, 1906.

Warrack, John — Tchaikovsky. London, 1973 — Tchaikovsky: Symphonies and Concertos. (BBC Music Guides: rev. ed. 1974) London

Weinstock, Herbert — Tchaikovsky. New York, 1943

Posters for concerts of Tchaikovsky's works

Contents

Chapter 1

Genius Aroused

'In you I see the greatest, or rather the only, hope for our musical future' —
Herman Laroche

Whether he cared to admit it or not, Peter Ilyich Tchaikovsky was a
hypochondriac, a manic-depressive and a man who, until only a few
months before his death, was quite unable to come to terms with his
own nature. He was also, quite clearly, a genius; one of the greatest
composers ever to have lived, and an artist whose music conveys
the very spirit of 19th century Russia. Unlike Mozart or Schubert,
he was not an infant prodigy, nor was his family background
particularly musical. But from an early age Tchaikovsky's
extremely sensitive nature was apparent to those around him, and it
was this nature which was later to find expression in some of the
most personal and deeply-felt music ever to be committed to paper.
As a mature composer he was highly critical of his own work and
went out of his way to draw attention to what he considered to be
weaknesses in his own music. On more than one occasion during
his lifetime he deliberately destroyed entire scores. To this sensitive
and self-critical nature a third element must be added: he was
fiercely proud of his own nationality. 'I am Russian, *Russian*, in the
fullest sense of the word' he once declared, and strenuously resisted
any suggestion that his ancestors may have been Polish in origin.

He was born in Votinsk, in the Government of Vyatka, on 7 May
1840, the second child of Ilya Petrovitch Tchaikovsky who was at
that time manager of the important Kamsko-Votinsk iron mines, a
post which gave him considerable status within the community. By
all accounts he was a charming, unassuming man, not particularly
gifted or intelligent, but capable and hard-working — all of them
qualities one would expect to find in a successful middle-class
government official in Russia, as elsewhere. The composer's
younger brother, Modest, once described their father's character as
'sympathetic, jovial and straightforward'. In 1833, Ilya had married
for the second time and had taken as his wife Alexandra Assier, who
came of French Huguenot stock. Her grandfather, like many of his
fellow-countrymen, had fled the Revolution and settled in Russia.

1

Alexandra Assier, the
Composer's mother

Alexandra's father, André Assier, was a state councillor of some distinction, although he was by nature a nervous and impulsive man. Both characteristics lend substance to the view that there was a history of epilepsy in Alexandra's family, and it is known that her grandfather actually suffered epileptic fits from time to time. At the time of her marriage she was 20 years old and has been described as 'tall and distinguished; not precisely handsome, but with wonderfully expressive eyes'. Educated at a girls' orphanage, she spoke both French and German fluently and was a pianist and singer of moderate ability. These modest accomplishments were quite normal for girls of her social class at that time, and it would be mistaken to assume that they had any direct bearing on young Peter's own musical development. We do know, however, that he was deeply attached to his mother and that she had a very profound influence on her son during his early years.

When he was four years old, Tchaikovsky's mother decided to engage a governess for her niece Lydia, who lived with the family, and her eldest son Nikolay. Her choice fell on a young French girl, Fanny Durbach, and as soon as she took up her duties, Peter, already a 'winning and precociously intelligent child', insisted on sharing all the lessons, although this had not been his mother's original intention. Peter seems to have received more than his fair share of Fanny's attention and affection, although this was perhaps inevitable as he was by far the youngest of her charges. At all events, she has left valuable recollections of Tchaikovsky's early childhood: his clothes, we are told, were

always in disorder. Either he had stained them in his absent-mindedness, or buttons were missing, or his hair was only half-brushed.

Illya Petrovitch
Tchaikovsky, the
Composer's father

Fanny herself was not in the least musical, and she did her best to restrict the amount of time the boy spent at the piano, and to encourage his early attempts at literature. Of his academic ability, and of his temperament, she has this to say:

At lessons no child was more industrious or quicker to understand; in playtime none was so full of fun . . . his sensitivity was extreme, therefore I had to be very careful how I treated him. A trifle wounded him deeply. He was as brittle as porcelain. With him there would be no question of punishment: the least criticism or reproof of a kind that would pass lightly over other children would upset him alarmingly . . .

On one occasion, during his recreation hour, Fanny found young Peter turning over the pages of his atlas. Coming to a map of Europe, he smothered Russia with kisses and spat on all the other

The house in Votinsk where
Tchaikovsky was born

countries. Fanny, who was clearly a level-headed and sensible girl,
describes what followed:

> When I told him he ought to be ashamed of such behaviour, that it was
> wicked to hate his fellow men . . . and that he was spitting on his own
> Fanny, who was a Frenchwoman, he replied at once: "There is no need to
> scold me. Didn't you see me cover France with my hand first?"
> 'As our leisure hours were few, I insisted on devoting them to physical
> exercise. But often I met with some opposition from Pierre, who would go
> straight from his lessons to the piano. Otherwise, he was obedient and
> generally enjoyed romping with his sisters. Left to himself, he preferred to
> play the piano, or to read and write poetry.

Fanny's attempts to moderate her pupil's enthusiasm for music
could not have been made easier by the presence in the household
not only of a piano, but also a remarkable instrument known as an
orchestrion. This consisted of a large number of organ pipes of
various lengths and sizes, designed to represent the instruments of
an orchestra, which were controlled either by pinned cylinders as in
a conventional musical box, or by perforated paper rolls.
Tchaikovsky himself acknowledged that 'he owed his first musical
impressions to this instrument' and, in particular, his 'passionate
worship' of Mozart, arias from whose *Don Giovanni* were to be

3

Orchestrions, which
consisted of an elaborate
series of organ pipes worked
either by pinned cylinders
or perforated rolls, were
designed to imitate the
instruments of an orchestra

found in the collection of mechanical music, as well as selections
from the works of Bellini, Donizetti and Rossini. With his remarkable ear, he was able to pick out with great accuracy on the piano
tunes that he had heard on the orchestrion, and not long after his
fifth birthday it was decided to engage a piano tutor to give him
more formal musical instruction. Her name was Maria Markovna
Palchikova, of whom nothing is known except that she was a freed
serf. Within three years, Tchaikovsky was able to sight-read as well
as his young tutor.

We learn from Fanny that music always excited and unsettled the
boy. One night, after a party in the house, she found him sitting up
in bed, his eyes feverishly bright, crying 'Oh, this music, this
music! Save me from it!' In an attempt to calm him, Fanny
explained that the music had long since stopped and that the house

4

Father of the composer in the 1830's

Mother of the composer in the 1830's

Autograph copy of a poem written by the eight-year-old Tchaikovsky

was now completely quiet. 'It is here, it is here,' he replied, pointing at his head. 'I can't get rid of it: it won't leave me in peace.'

In the words of the late M. D. Calvocoressi, Fanny Durbach 'exercised a wholesome influence upon Tchaikovsky's excitable and morbidly sensitive disposition'. Her teaching ability was also of a high order, because by the age of six Peter could speak both French and German fluently. Undoubtedly his mother also played her part in this early linguistic achievement, but the fact remains that in Fanny Durbach she had made an excellent choice of governess for her young family. But unhappily — perhaps disastrously — for young Peter, the affection and the sense of security which she was able to provide were soon to come to an abrupt end.

In 1848, Tchaikovsky's father, who now enjoyed a rank equivalent to that of a major-general, decided to resign from government service in order to take up a new, more lucrative and — as it turned out — totally illusory appointment in Moscow. The loyal and devoted Fanny was dismissed, and on September 26 the uprooted family set out from Votinsk only to discover, on their arrival in Moscow twelve days later, that the coveted post had been snatched from Ilya Petrovitch by an unscrupulous friend. To make matters worse, cholera was raging in the city, and it was decided immediately to take the family on to St Petersburg, where both Nikolay and Peter were sent to a fashionable boarding school. Here they were teased as country yokels, and their unsympathetic teachers worked them to an absurdly excessive extent. To add to their misery, both boys quickly succumbed to a measles epidemic.

Nikolay made a normal recovery but Peter, distressed by his strange new surroundings and the loss of Fanny's care and attention, appeared not to respond to medical treatment. His condition was diagnosed by the doctor as 'spinal brain' disease, and a complete rest of at least six months was prescribed. Meanwhile, Ilya Petrovitch had found himself a suitable post as manager of some private mines not far from the Siberian border, at Alapayesk and Nizhny-Nevyansk. Once again the family was uprooted and all except Nikolay, for whom it had been decided that he should stay at the boarding school in St Petersburg, set off for their new, remote home beyond the Urals.

During this period of upheaval and change, Tchaikovsky's education had been left in the uncertain hands of his half-sister Zinaida, herself little more than a child. For a short time the services of a piano tutor, Filippov, were engaged, but the lessons were quickly abandoned when the boy fell ill. Now, in addition to all the feelings of insecurity and bewilderment brought about by the constant changes of plan and movement from place to place, Peter had to endure pangs of separation from his brother Nikolay, to whom he

Fanny Durbach

5

The Tchaikovsky Family in 1848 (the Composer is standing next to his mother on the far left)

was devoted. Small wonder that despite a steady improvement in his physical condition, he grew increasingly morose, irritable and — much to his mother's annoyance and concern — lazy. 'He has grown idle, learns nothing and often makes me cry with vexation', she wrote to Fanny Durbach, who was now happily settled in another post.

Matters improved towards the end of 1849 with the appointment of a new governess, Anastasia Petrova, under whose careful supervision Peter resumed his studies with growing enthusiasm. In a further report to Fanny Durbach, his mother declared that he was 'becoming more reasonable'. To see her son slowly regaining his earlier composure while remaining highly introverted and self-preoccupied, must have been a considerable relief to Peter's mother, who soon had other matters to attend to. In May 1850 she gave birth to twin boys, who were christened Anatol and Modest: 'angels descended to earth' as Peter described them in a letter to Fanny Durbach. Despite the difference in their ages, Modest was to become Tchaikovsky's most devoted confidant in later years.

Shortly after the arrival of his twin brothers, it was decided that Peter should resume his formal education, this time at the preparatory department of the School of Jurisprudence in St. Petersburg. He was entered as a boarder, and as the family home was such a vast distance from the capital his mother arranged with old friends, Modest Alekseyevich Vakar and his wife, that they should act as

6

Peter's guardians during his stay in the city. In October 1850 Peter and his mother set off on their long journey to St. Petersburg where, as a special treat, she took him to a performance of Glinka's *A Life for the Tsar*, which made a profound impression on him. The carefully-laid plans seemed to be working smoothly, but when the time came for Peter's mother to return home he was overcome by grief and hysteria. It was a painful and terrifying experience which was to remain with him for the rest of his life, as his brother Modest records:

When the actual moment of parting came he completely lost his self-control and, clinging wildly to his mother, refused to let her go. Neither kisses nor words of comfort nor the promise to return soon were of any avail. He saw nothing, heard nothing, but hung upon her as though he was part and parcel of her beloved presence. It became necessary to carry off the poor child by force and to hold him fast until his mother had driven away. Even then he broke loose and, with a cry of despair, ran after the carriage and clung to one of the wheels as though he would bring the vehicle to a standstill. To his life's end Tchaikovsky could never recall this hour without a shiver of horror.

Moscow in 1848

But that horror was not to end even there. Within a month,
scarlet fever broke out at Peter's school and Vakar took him in at
once to stay with his family until it was safe to return. A few days
later, Vakar's eldest son caught the infection and died on November
24. Peter himself escaped, and although the bereaved family did
everything in their power to assure him that he was in no way
responsible for the tragedy, he was overcome by guilt and remorse,
and begged his parents to remove him from the house. They wisely
insisted on his returning to school as soon as the outbreak had run
its course.

Unhappy, depressed and homesick as he undoubtedly was, Peter
responded to the routine of the school and made good progress in
his studies throughout the following year. In May 1852, Ilya
Petrovitch retired, and with the help of a government pension and
his own modest savings he was able to move his family once again,
this time out of near exile beyond the Urals to the warmth and
gaiety of St. Petersburg itself. Tchaikovsky was overjoyed to be re-
united with his family, and there was further cause for rejoicing
when the results of his entrance examination for the School of
Jurisprudence were published. He had done extremely well, and in
high spirits the whole Tchaikovsky family spent a happy and
delightful holiday that summer on a country estate not far from St.
Petersburg.

At the start of the new academic year Tchaikovsky took up his
place in the senior school, where he quickly made new friends.
Among them was the future poet Alexander Apukhtin, who was to
provide him with numerous texts and verses over the years, and
Vladimir Adamov, a great lover of music who became a senior

8

The School of Jurisprudence in St. Petersburg

Group of students from the School of Jurisprudence, 1859, with Tchaikovsky in front, seventh from the left

The characters Zerlina and Don Giovanni from Mozart's opera *Don Giovanni*

official in the Ministry of Justice. Peter continued to do moderately well at his studies at the School of Jurisprudence despite the fact that the course of instruction placed more emphasis, not unnaturally, on the development of literary rather than of musical ability.

For eighteen months or more, Peter's life was far happier and more tranquil than it had been at any time since the first, disastrous family uprooting and the departure of Fanny Durbach. But in July 1854 came another shattering blow. Tchaikovsky's mother contracted cholera and died. The effect of this disaster on the fourteen-year-old boy can only be surmised, for there are no letters or writings of any kind from Tchaikovsky himself — at least, none appears to have survived. It was only some two and a half years after the event that he could bring himself to write to Fanny Durbach:

Four months after Zinaida's marriage my mother was taken ill with cholera. Thanks to the care of her doctor she rallied, but not for long. Three days later she was taken from us without even time to bid us goodbye.

Tchaikovsky wrote his first known composition the month following his mother's death: *Valse dediée a m-lle Anastasia* for his former governess.

During that same summer he had also considered writing a one-act opera *Hyperbole* to a libretto by the poet Olkhovsky, but the project came to nothing. With one or two exceptions, his friends were not particularly musical, although he was from time to time encouraged by his aunt to play and to sing. By all accounts he had an extremely fine singing voice, and she put before him much of the popular operatic music of the day together with a full vocal score of *Don Giovanni*. Many years later, in 1878, Tchaikovsky wrote:

The music of *Don Giovanni* was the first to make a deep impression on me. It awoke a spiritual ecstasy which was afterwards to bear fruit. With its help I penetrated into that world of artistic beauty where only great genius abides. It is due to Mozart that I have devoted my life to music. He gave me the impulse to all my efforts, and made me love it above all else in the world.

At the School of Jurisprudence Peter was able to study singing under Lomakin, and the piano with Bekker. He also received lessons from Kundinger, an eminent German pianist who had made his home in St. Petersburg. Although he was impressed by his pupil's gift for improvisation, Kundinger advised Ilya Petrovitch not to allow his son to follow a musical career:

. . . in the first place, I saw no signs of genius in Tchaikovsky, and secondly because in my experience the lot of a musician in Russia at that time was an onerous one.

In later years, Kundinger admitted his error with disarming integrity:

If I had had any idea of what he was to become I should have kept a diary of our lessons. But I must admit, to my great embarrassment, that at no time did it occur to me that Tchaikovsky had in him the stuff of a musician . . . Certainly he was gifted, he had a good ear and memory, an excellent touch, but apart from that there was nothing — absolutely nothing — that suggested a composer or even a fine performer. Nothing remarkable, nothing phenomenal . . .

At about this time, when Tchaikovsky was sixteen, a rather more dubious relationship was established with a singing master named Luigi Piccioli, an outrageous character who dyed his hair, painted his face and defiantly claimed to be no older than fifty years of age ('cruel tongues did not hesitate to assert that he would never see seventy again', wrote Modest). He declared that he loathed all music except that of 'the great Italian melodists', and under his influence Italian opera became, for a time, Tchaikovsky's main musical concern.

Apart from these diversions, Tchaikovsky spent his years at the School of Jurisprudence coming to grips with, among other things, the science of mathematics, but distinguishing himself in no particular subject. After a promising start at the school he had lapsed into a comfortable mediocrity, and by the time of his graduation — shortly after his nineteenth birthday in 1859 — he occupied thirteenth position in his class. On leaving school he took up a post as clerk, first-class, in the Ministry of Justice. His career as a minor official was as undistinguished as the latter part of his academic career, although he did manage to get himself promoted to a position of senior assistant to the chief clerk after nine months of service. The main compensations of his routine duties were a sense of independence and a small, but very useful, salary. He lost no time in launching himself into St. Petersburg society, at whose gatherings both his good looks and his talent at the keyboard were fully appreciated. He became something of a fashionable dandy, and he spent many of his evenings at either the opera or the ballet. He felt himself to be far more at home in the theatre than in the daunting corridors of the Ministry.

For reasons which are by no means clear it was his father who, in March 1861, re-kindled thoughts in Tchaikovsky's head that he might take up music as a full-time career. This is revealed in a letter written to his sister Alexandra, who had recently married the son of

Luigi Piccioli

The Composer's father with the twins Modest and Anatol

a renowned revolutionary, Lev Davidov, and had settled in Kamenka in the Province of Kiev.

Father declared that it was not too late for me to become an artist. If only that were true! But it's like this — even if I actually had any talent, it can hardly be developed now. They've made an official of me, though a poor one. I am doing my best to improve and to attend to my duties more conscientiously. At the same time, I am to study thorough-bass.

These studies gave him the confidence he so badly needed: another letter to Alexandra, written some months later, reveals far greater optimism:

I am studying thorough-bass and making good progress. Who knows, perhaps in three years' time you'll be listening to my operas and singing my arias!

By the end of 1861, in December, he went even further:

You will agree that with my rather exceptional talents (I hope you will not mistake this for bragging) it seems foolish not to try my chances in this

11

Lev Davidov and the
Composer's 'Beloved' sister
Alexandra

direction. I dread only my own easy-going nature. In the end my indolence
will conquer: but if not then I promise you I shall do something. Luckily,
it is not yet too late.

The teaching of thorough-bass continued long after it ceased to
have any practical bearing on the art of composition, and certainly
by the middle of the 19th century it had become a term which
would have been applied to the teaching of harmony as a whole.
The public lessons which Tchaikovsky attended were organised by
the Russian Musical Society, a body which had been recently
established by the Grand Duchess Elena Pavlovna (an aunt of Tsar
Nicholas II) and her young protégé Anton Rubinstein (1830-94), a

Nikolay Zaremba

distinguished pianist and composer. It was during their travels together in Europe some ten years earlier that they determined to set up a permanent society to encourage both the study and performance of music in Russia — a country which, at that time, treated musicians with a certain amount of indifference. On her return to her native land, Elena Pavlovna successfully obtained her nephew's Imperial approval for the project, and the Russian Musical Society formally opened its doors in September 1859 at the home of the Grand Duchess, the Mikhailovsky Palace.

Tchaikovsky's teacher at the Russian Musical Society was Nikolay Zaremba (1821-79), an ardent classicist and an adherent of the German school of music based on the theories of Adolf Marx. The budding young composer responded to the new challenge with great enthusiasm and discarding his role as a man about town, he became instead a diligent and hard-working student. In this way he at last found a natural outlet for his talent and except for a brief period during the early part of 1862, when he forced himself to concentrate on his official duties at the Ministry in the hope of further promotion, music became his major preoccupation.

Meanwhile, the Russian Musical Society prospered. Encouraged by their initial success, the Grand Duchess and the pianist-composer set about acquiring larger premises and guarantees of further financial support to enable them to establish a fully-fledged Conservatoire. The Tsar, impressed by what he had seen, not only willingly gave his consent but also — more importantly — his backing, and in due course the Conservatoire opened in a luxurious house on the banks of the River Neva, with Rubinstein, naturally enough, as its first Director. Peter Ilyich Tchaikovsky enrolled as one of its first students, continuing his studies under Zaremba of counterpoint and church music and, for good measure, also taking lessons in the playing of the flute, piano and organ. Just two days after joining the Conservatoire he wrote a further letter to Alexandra:

The Tsar Alexander II

I have come to the conclusion that sooner or later I shall give up my present occupation for music. Do not imagine I dream of being a great artist . . . I only feel that I must do work for which I have a vocation. Whether I become a celebrated composer or merely a struggling music teacher — it's all the same. In either event my conscience will be clear, and I shall no longer have the right to grumble at my lot. Of course, I shall not resign my present position until I am sure that I am no longer a clerk, but a musician.

But for Tchaikovsky the moment of decision was much closer than he was prepared to admit, even to his sister. Late in 1863 he was passed over for promotion, and promptly resigned his clerical post in the Ministry of Justice. Undoubtedly he was encouraged to

Herman Laroche

take this course of action by a number of friends who expressed great confidence in his musical abilities. Prominent among these was Herman Laroche (1845-1904) who, in spite of being five years Tchaikovsky's junior, had become a close friend since their first meeting at the Conservatoire and passionately believed in his talent and his potential. Such perspicacity was amply rewarded later in Laroche's career, for he became one of Russia's most distinguished music critics. But he was not alone in his view of Tchaikovsky: many of the teachers at the Conservatoire shared his opinion, although they probably expressed themselves in more guarded terms. One of them, indeed, is known to have chided the young composer for not working 'more fastidiously when obviously possessing so much talent.' Anton Rubinstein himself, the severest judge of all, excused Tchaikovsky his compulsory piano lessons to allow him to devote more time to theory and composition. Later he recalled that his student worked

. . . in an amazing manner. Once in composition class I told him to write out contrapuntal variations on a given theme, and mentioned that in this sort of work not only quality but quantity was important. I thought he might write about twelve variations. Not at all: at the next class he gave me over two hundred.

Neither enjoyed the other's music to any great extent, but as the relationship between Rubinstein and Tchaikovsky matured they came to regard each other with a deep respect. It was Rubinstein's opinion and, hopefully, his approval that Tchaikovsky valued above all others.

The family had been kept very fully informed of Tchaikovsky's decision to take up music as a full-time career. Before his departure from the Ministry, he wrote to Alexandra, in a letter dated 27 April 1863:—

I know that I shall be a good musician and that I shall be able to earn my daily bread. The professors are satisfied with me, and say that with the necessary zeal I shall do well. I do not tell you this in a boastful spirit (it is not my nature), only to speak to you openly and without any false modesty.

I cherish a dream — to come to you for a whole year after my studies are finished and to compose a great work in your quiet surroundings. After that — out into the world.

Alexandra's reactions are not recorded, but his brother Nikolay, now a successful official in the provinces, was horrified to hear that he had entered such an 'undignified' profession and observed, with sarcasm, that he 'would never become another Glinka'. To which Tchaikovsky replied with both moderation and confidence:

I may never become another Glinka, but the day will come when you will be proud of me.

14

Tchaikovsky in 1862

Tchaikovsky's diploma from the St. Petersburg Conservatoire

The Moscow Conservatoire during the 1860's

In sharp contrast to Nikolay's scorn, Ilya Petrovitch did everything he could to help his son. With a modest pension and two thirteen-year-old twins to support his means were limited, and he could offer only a small room and the promise of some food. Tchaikovsky accepted gratefully. Hardship of this kind no longer troubled him — indeed, he revelled in it. His fashionable clothes became shabby and he grew his hair long, no doubt in emulation of his idol Rubinstein. He earned a meagre income by giving a few piano lessons but, as Modest remembers,

'. . . at no time in his life was he so cheerful and serene. In a small room which held only a bed and a writing table, he started bravely on his new and laborious existence.'

Both Rubinstein and Zaremba were cast very firmly in the classical mould, and it is therefore not surprising that Tchaikovsky's early compositions at the Conservatoire turned out to be little more than competent academic exercises. But his natural gift for orchestration and his disregard for conventional musical form could not long be suppressed, especially now he had had a chance of learning how Wagner, Liszt and Berlioz used orchestral forces in a series of concerts promoted by the Russian Musical Society. During the summer of 1864, spent in Trostinets as the guest of Prince Golistan, Tchaikovsky broke free from academic bonds and composed a piece in his own highly individual and characteristic style. It was an Overture based on a play which he much admired called *The Storm*, written by Alexander Ostrovsky (1823-86).

When the Conservatoire re-convened it was customary for work done during the vacation to be submitted to the Director for his inspection. As it happened, Tchaikovsky fell ill shortly before he was due to return to St. Petersburg, so he asked his friend Laroche to hand in his completed score of *The Storm*. It was well that he did so, for it was the unfortunate Laroche who received the full force of Rubinstein's anger. Here was not the expected classical exercise, but a mature attempt at dramatic programme music. To compound the felony, orchestral forces were employed which were strictly forbidden to mere students of the Conservatoire. It was, as events turned out, the first of many such clashes between Rubinstein and his pupil. The work itself was not published until after Tchaikovsky's death, which explains its high opus number (76), and although not entirely convincing it is nevertheless an early testimony to the genius of its composer.

Undaunted, Tchaikovsky continued his studies and, in an attempt to placate Rubinstein, wrote two further overtures in a much less unconventional form. The first, in the key of C minor, used material from *The Storm* while the second, in F major, was

Tchaikovsky's 'musical god', Wolfgang Amadeus Mozart (an unfinished painting by Lange)

The Rubinstein brothers,
Nikolay and Anton

considered suitable to be performed by the orchestra of the Conservatoire with Tchaikovsky himself conducting. He also started work on a string quartet in B flat major, of which only one movement survives, and completed a set of dances which he called *Dances of the Serving Maids*. These were given their first performance in the summer of 1865 at an open-air concert under the baton of none other than Johann Strauss II. They were an immediate success and a source of great encouragement to the hard-pressed composer. He was over-tired as a result of incessant work, and his financial position was now desperate. In addition, his eyes were giving him trouble.

Further encouragement was, however, on the way. Five years earlier Nikolay Rubinstein (1835-81), Anton's brother, had founded a branch of the Russian Musical Society in Moscow. It met with considerable success, and plans were now laid for its expansion. Nikolay wrote to St. Petersburg asking Anton to recommend a suitable candidate for the post of a tutor of harmony, and Rubinstein put forward Tchaikovsky's name. An offer was made, conditional upon his graduating from the St. Petersburg Conservatoire, which Tchaikovsky accepted, in spite of the very meagre monthly salary of 50 roubles (about £5) which the post carried.

16

For his graduation piece Rubinstein insisted that Tchaikovsky should compose a cantata to Schiller's *Ode to Joy* — scarcely an original choice of text. However, the young composer set about his task and the work, which was scored for soloists, chorus and orchestra, was performed during a prize-giving ceremony at the Conservatoire on 12 January 1866 before a distinguished panel. Two days later, a *viva voce* was held in public for all intending graduates, but in a fit of nervous anxiety Tchaikovsky failed to present himself. Rubinstein was furious, and threatened to withhold Tchaikovsky's diploma: forty-eight hours later, however, his temper cooled, and he relented, much to the young composer's relief.

The cantata provoked a storm of critical abuse. Rubinstein himself demanded its revision; Serov (1820-71), an influential composer at that time, expressed stern disapproval, and Cui (1835-1918), one of the leading nationalist composers, hurled abuse at the work for a period of several months. Only the faithful Laroche was convinced:

Tchaikovsky in 1863

'I tell you frankly that I consider yours is the greatest musical talent to which Russia can look forward in the future. Stronger and more original than Balakirev, loftier and more creative than Serov, far more refined than Rimsky-Korsakov, I see in you the greatest, or rather the only, hope for our musical future. Your own original creations will probably not make their appearance for another five years. But these ripe and classic works will surpass everything we have heard since Glinka. To sum up: I do not honour you so much for what you have done, as for what the force and vitality of your genius will one day accomplish. The proofs you have given so far are but solemn pledges to outdo all your contemporaries.'

A few days later Tchaikovsky left his family and friends in St. Petersburg to take up his new appointment in Moscow. His mood was despondent. His future seemed precarious. But as Laroche had correctly perceived, his genius had been aroused.

Chapter 2

Early Failures

'You are needed by us . . . by Russia' — Nikolay Rubinstein

When Tchaikovsky arrived in Moscow to take up his new appointment at what had now become the Conservatoire, the auspices were
not good. As so often in the past he was overcome by melancholia,
homesickness and depression, and was in no mood to respond in
any positive way to his new surroundings. It says much for the
patience, understanding and tolerance of his new Director, Nikolay
Rubinstein, that this transition from student to teacher was made
relatively painless. Tchaikovsky was very relieved to find him so
kind and sympathetic, with no trace of his brother's highly un-
approachable manner. Although he was Tchaikovsky's senior by
only five years, Nikolay Rubinstein treated his new member of staff
as a father might treat a son. 'He looks after me like a nurse,'
Tchaikovsky wrote to the twins. Not only did Rubinstein offer him
every hospitality, insisting that he share his house, but he also
presented him with half-a-dozen new shirts and ordered a frock-coat
from his own tailor. Rubinstein's warm welcome and his constant
enthusiasm and encouragement were to have the most profound
effect upon Tchaikovsky.

Other important friendships were formed during these early days
in Moscow. Two men in particular were to become life-long friends
of the young composer. The first was Constantine Albrecht (1836-
93), who held the important office of Inspector of the Conservatoire. Secondly, there was Nikolay Kashkin (1839-1920) who was a
professor at the Conservatoire and a close friend of Laroche: he was
destined to become an eminent critic in his own right. In addition,
Tchaikovsky was fortunate enough to make the acquaintance of his
future publisher P. I. Jurgenson (1836-1903), who was an astute
and enterprising man, prominent in the musical life of Moscow and
a passionate believer in the future of Russian music. As the years
unfolded, it was Jurgenson who published by far the greater part of
Tchaikovsky's output.

Despite his initial misgivings, Tchaikovsky started his lecturing

Peter Jurgenson,
Tchaikovsky's future
publisher

General view of the
Kremlin in Moscow

career and before long surprised himself at his growing
competence. On 19 February 1866 he wrote to Alexandra:

I am gradually becoming used to Moscow, although sometimes I feel
very lonely. My classes are successful, to my great astonishment: my
nervousness is vanishing completely and I am gradually assuming the airs
of a professor. My homesickness is also wearing off, but Moscow is still a
strange place and it will be long before I can contemplate, without horror,
the thought of remaining here for years — perhaps for ever.

In fact he spent his time rather more enjoyably than this letter
suggests. Not only was he deriving great amusement from reading
Dickens's *Pickwick Papers*, but he also spent a great deal of his
spare time in Nikolay's company at the English Club where, undoubtedly, the seeds of his heavy drinking in later years were sown.
So far as his compositional work was concerned, he confined himself to revising the two student overtures written during the
previous year. Both Rubinstein brothers roundly condemned the C
minor overture, and many years later Tchaikovsky himself
described the work as 'dreadful rubbish'. The manuscript was
eventually lost, and did not come to light until 1922, when it was
published for the first time. On the other hand, the F major overture fared very much better: Tchaikovsky re-worked it for full
orchestra, and on 16 March it received its first performance under

19

Nikolay Rubinstein. As always, Tchaikovsky reported back to his family, this time in a letter to the twins:

I was unanimously recalled, but more flattering still was the ovation I received at the supper which Rubinstein gave after the concert, when he proposed my health amid renewed applause. I go into these details because it is my first public success, and consequently very gratifying.

Suitably encouraged, Tchaikovsky felt that he was ready to undertake his first major project, and started working on sketches for a symphony in the key of G minor: as events were soon to prove he was ready neither physically nor mentally for such a task. Within a matter of days came Cui's scathing press review of the graduation Cantata in which, among other things, he described the composer as 'altogether weak'. Tchaikovsky had not yet learned to defend himself against music critics and fellow-composers, and took these strictures very much to heart. In a letter to a friend he confessed:

When I read this terrible judgement I hardly know what happened to me. Everything went black before my eyes, my head began to spin and I ran out of the cafe like a madman. I was not aware of what I was doing or where I was going. The whole day long, I wandered the streets, repeating to myself 'I am sterile . . . I am insignificant . . . I shall never amount to anything . . . I have no talent.

However much one may feel that Tchaikovsky over-reacted to harsh criticism, it must be said to his credit that he did not take refuge only in self-pity. As he was to do so often in the future, he threw himself into his work with re-doubled zeal, drafting and re-drafting passages for his first symphony both day and night. By the end of April he was, physically, in a state of near-collapse, plagued by insomnia and severe pains in the head, which he referred to as 'apoplectic strokes'. He described his condition at that time in a letter which he wrote to Anatol:

My nerves are altogether shaken. The causes are:—
1) The symphony, which does not sound at all satisfactory;
2) Rubinstein and Tarnovsky have discovered that I am easily startled, and amuse themselves by giving me all manner of shocks all day long;
3) I cannot shake off the conviction that I shall not live long, and that I shall leave my symphony unfinished.
I long for the summer and for Kamenka as for the Promised Land, and there I hope to find rest and peace, and to forget all my troubles . . . I hate mankind in the mass, and I should be delighted to retire into a wilderness with very few inhabitants.

Charles Dickens, one of Tchaikovsky's favourite authors

20

Tchaikovsky's first scathing
critic, César Cui (1835-1918)

Mikhail Ivanovich Glinka
(1804-57)

News from St. Petersburg that his F major Overture had been given a successful performance under Anton Rubinstein lifted his morale for a time, and he was able to write to Alexandra saying that his health was much improved. He still attached the utmost importance to the approval of St. Petersburg audiences and to recognition by Anton Rubinstein himself. His recovery was, however, short-lived. The proposed trip to Kamenka, by which he had set so much store, had to be abandoned because the roads were impassable, and it was arranged instead that he should spend the summer months at Myather, with his sister's mother-in-law Alexandra Davidova and her daughters Vera and Elizabeta.

At first, the peace and beauty of the countryside acted as a tonic, and he spent his time happily going through the scores of the Schumann symphonies and, especially, Mendelssohn's *Italian Symphony*, all of which had recently been published in Russia. But when he resumed work on his own symphony, all the alarming symptoms returned. At the end of July a doctor was called in. After a careful examination, he declared that Tchaikovsky was 'on the verge of madness', and ordered a complete rest. The terrified composer complied at once, and undertook never to work again at night.

As a result of this restriction in his working hours and the inherent difficulties in the work itself, Tchaikovsky was not able to complete the symphony during the summer months, as he had hoped. Nevertheless he sent the manuscript in its unfinished form to Anton Rubinstein and Zaremba before his return to Moscow. Any expectations he may have had that the Russian Musical Society would give the work its first performance were immediately dashed when both musicians rejected the score, saying that it required extensive revision and that it was quite unworthy to be performed in its existing form. Such an unhelpful response from St. Petersburg made the prospect of his return to Moscow seem rather less daunting, and there at least good news awaited him. He found to his pleasure that his salary had been doubled ('I have money enough to spare', he wrote jubilantly to the twins), and that the Conservatoire was shortly to move into larger premises. The new building was formally opened on September 13 and after an inaugural banquet Tchaikovsky, determined that the first music to be heard in the new concert hall should be that of Glinka (1803-57), performed, from memory, at the piano the overture *Russlan and Ludmilla*.

Another respite from the anxiety he felt about the symphony was a commission from Nikolay Rubinstein to write a festival overture based on the Danish national anthem, to celebrate the forthcoming marriage of the Tsarevitch to Princess Dagmar of Denmark. The work was dedicated to the Tsarevitch himself, and received its first

21

Alexander Borodin
(1833- 87)

performance during a ceremonial visit which the royal couple made to Moscow in November. The bridegroom expressed his gratitude by presenting Tchaikovsky with an ostentatious pair of gold cuff-links, which he promptly sold to a colleague.

By the end of November, his first Symphony was complete and Nikolay Rubinstein offered to give the work its first performance. But Tchaikovsky remained obsessed with the idea that St. Petersburg should hear it first, and grudgingly allowed only the scherzo to be given in Moscow, which met with little success. Having made all the revisions demanded by his formidable professors, Tchaikovsky sent the work to St. Petersburg for their approval. Once again they turned it down, although the two middle movements were passed as 'being fit for performance' and were, in fact, played at a concert given by the Russian Musical Society on 23 February 1867. They were not a success. Now, thoroughly disillusioned by St. Petersburg audiences and the critical judgement of both Rubinstein and Zaremba, Tchaikovsky scrapped all the revisions and stood firmly by his original version. To his disappointment, however, he had to wait a whole year before the symphony was performed in its entirety.

Fortunately, he was already engrossed in a new venture, an opera based on a play called *The Voyevoda*,* also written by Ostrovsky. He had first mentioned the project in a letter written to Anatol the previous November, and was both pleased and flattered when Ostrovsky agreed to prepare a libretto. Early in March 1867 the first act was ready, and Tchaikovsky started to work on it almost immediately. However, the collaboration was doomed to failure.

With extraordinary carelessness Tchaikovsky lost the playwright's text, and Ostrovsky was forced to re-write the first Act from memory. Then, hearing nothing from the composer, he began to lose patience and gradually the collaboration faltered. By the summer, which Tchaikovsky spent at Hapsal with Alexandra Davidova and her family, it had collapsed altogether but, quite undaunted, the composer decided to complete the libretto himself. It was a summer which began under the happiest of auspices. Gone were all the neurotic symptoms which had so distressed him while writing the symphony: he was even able to complete a set of three piano pieces which he dedicated to Vera Davidova under the title *Souvenir de Hapsal* (Op 2). But self-pity was never far below the surface, as this letter to Alexandra reveals:

I am already very tired of life . . . I dream of a calm, heavenly, serene existence which I experience only when I am in your company. Be sure of this: you will have to devote some of your maternal devotion to your tired

* A *Voyevode* was a senior official, roughly the equivalent of a State Governor in the USA, or a Lord Lieutenant of a county in Great Britain.

Tchaikovsky in 1868

old brother. Perhaps you may think that such a frame of mind naturally leads a man to think about matrimony. No, my dear future companion!

My weariness has made me *too indolent* to form new ties, *too indolent* to raise a family, *too indolent* to take upon myself the responsibility of a wife and children. In short, marriage to me is unthinkable.

These were perhaps the first rumblings of a volcano which finally erupted in 1877, when his inner torment forced Tchaikovsky into a disastrous marriage. Of his homosexual love affairs at this time there is no direct evidence, although later correspondence suggests that he was already following his natural (some, even now, would say unnatural) inclinations. He was extremely anxious about gossip which was already circulating about his sexual tastes and, in an attempt to avert scandal, he embarked upon an elaborate cover-up which he sustained for many years. During this summer of 1867 his unwillingness to come to terms with his homosexuality had not yet developed into the self-inflicted torture of later years, although he did allow himself to comment, perhaps half-jokingly, about a problem which would soon become, in his own words, his 'greatest obstacle to happiness'.

Later that same year (1867) there are a number of references in his letters to 'drunkenness', but despite the social activity which this presumably entailed he was able to complete *The Voyevoda* by December. Dances from the opera were separately performed by Nikolay Rubinstein shortly before the end of the year. According to Modest, they proved to be an 'undeniable success', which view is supported by the fact that they were given two further performances during the season. On 3 February 1868 however, there came the first major step forward in Tchaikovsky's composing career when his first symphony, which now carried the sub-title *Winter Daydreams,* received its first full performance in Moscow. 'Its success,' wrote Modest, 'surpassed all expectations.' Shortly afterwards, Tchaikovsky was persuaded to make his public début as a conductor: included among the pieces to be given at a charity concert were the dances from *The Voyevoda.* Kashkin later described what happened:

The renowned critic Stassov, by Repin

When I went behind the scenes to see how the *debutant* felt, he told me that to his great surprise he was not in the least nervous. When Tchaikovsky came on to the platform, however, I noticed that he was quite distraught. He came on timidly, as though he would have been glad to hide or to run away, and on mounting to the conductor's desk he looked a man who finds himself in some desperate situation. Apparently, his own composition was blotted out from his mind: he did not see the score in front of him, and gave all the leads at the wrong moment or to the wrong instruments. Fortunately, the orchestra knew the music so well that they paid no attention whatever to Tchaikovsky's beat but, laughing up their

23

Nikolay Rimsky-Korsakov
(1844-1908)

sleeves, they got through the dances very creditably. Afterwards, Peter Ilyich told me that, in his terror, he felt that his head would fall off his shoulders unless he held it tightly in position.

It was ten years before Tchaikovsky ventured to conduct in public again, and a further ten years after that before he finally overcame his fear of the podium.

Despite Tchaikovsky's inept performance, in both senses of the word, this charity concert was to have an important consequence. Among the works performed was the *Fantasia on Serbian Themes*, composed by Rimsky-Korsakov (1844-1908), which greatly impressed Tchaikovsky during the rehearsals. Within a few days of the concert itself a review appeared in a publication called the *Entr'acte* which praised the *Voyevoda* dances for 'their masterly conception', but condemned the *Fantasia on Serbian Themes* as 'colourless and inanimate'. Tchaikovsky was incensed, and came to the defence of his fellow-composer in a lengthy article published in the *Sovremennaya Letopis*. This caused a sensation, and brought Tchaikovsky into close and cordial contact with the 'New School' of Russian composers, of whom Rimsky-Korsakov was one, who virtually controlled the musical life of St. Petersburg. The movement was originally founded by Dargomizhsky (1813-69), with Glinka as its inspiration and the renowned critic Stassov (1824-1906) its principal champion. Known as *The Band*, or *Kuchka*, it also numbered among its members Balakirev (1836-1910), Cui, Borodin (1833-87) and Mussorgsky (1839-81). They passionately believed in writing Russian music, free of any Western influence, for the Russian people. They despised the Rubinsteins and their pupils for their unquestioned acceptance of Western ideas and, in turn, *The Band* was castigated by the Rubinstein camp. Tchaikovsky had himself earlier referred to the nationalists in contemptuous terms, describing them as the 'St. Petersburg amateurs'.

With the publication of his article, however, the situation changed dramatically, at least so far as Tchaikovsky was concerned. *The Band* were naturally delighted that a Rubinstein adherent should support, in such strong terms, the work of one of their most important members, and when Tchaikovsky arrived in St. Petersburg to spend Easter with his father he was warmly welcomed into their ranks. In a way that is characteristically Russian, the reconciliation actually took place around Dargomizhsky's deathbed. The breach was healed and *The Band* now became ardent champions of Tchaikovsky's music in the capital. In return, Tchaikovsky was sympathetic and sought their advice, but he did not fully commit himself to the cause. Indeed, in 1878 he was still able to write in these terms, in a letter to Mme. von Meck:

24

Mussorgsky (1839-81) a
painting by Repin

The St. Petersburg composers are very gifted, but they are all full of the
most horrible presumptuousness, and a purely amateur conviction regarding the superiority over all other musicians in the universe.

Whatever Tchaikovsky's innermost thoughts, publicly at least an
important reconciliation had taken place. The position is perhaps
best summed up in Modest's words:

The relations between Tchaikovsky and *The Band* may be compared
with those which exist between two friendly neighbouring states, each
leading its own existence, meeting on common ground, but keeping their
individual interests strictly apart.

Tchaikovsky spent the summer of 1868 in Paris in the company
of his favourite pupil and close friend Vladimir Shilovsky who was
the consumptive step-son of Begichev, Intendant of the Moscow
Imperial Theatres. Production standards at the Paris Opéra made a
deep impression on Tchaikovsky:

What earnest attention is given to every detail, no matter how insignificant, which goes to make up the general effect. We have no conception of
such performances.

On his return to Moscow in September he learned that his salary
had again been increased, and that *The Voyevoda* was being
prepared for performance at the Bolshoi Theatre the following
month.
However, rehearsals for the opera were postponed at the end of
September at Tchaikovsky's own request. He considered that the
presence of a visiting Italian opera company in Moscow would
prove too great a distraction for the Bolshoi orchestra and chorus.

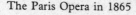

The Paris Opera in 1865

25

Désirée Artôt

But this was not the only reason. On the opening of the Italian company's season at the Bolshoi on 23 September, Tchaikovsky attended a performance of Rossini's *Otello*, which was distinguished neither for its staging nor for its singing. Laroche takes up the story:

The one exception was a woman of thirty, not good-looking, but with a passionate and expressive face, who had just reached the climax of her art. Désirée Artôt, a daughter of the celebrated horn-player Artôt and a niece of the still more renowned violinist, had been trained by Pauline Viardot-Garcia. Her voice was powerful, and adapted to express dramatic pathos

26

. . . It is not too much to say that in the whole world of music, in the entire range of lyrical emotion, there was not a single idea or a single form of which this admirable artist could not give a poetical interpretation . . . I have said that Artôt was not good-looking. At the same time, without recourse to artificial aids, her charm was so great that she won all hearts and turned all heads, as though she had been the loveliest of women.

Among the hearts she won and the heads she turned on that opening night were undoubtedly those of Peter Ilyich Tchaikovsky. He fell madly in love with her. Désirée Artôt became an obsession: work on a new symphonic poem, *Fatum*, was thrust aside, and in its place he wrote a piano piece, *Romance in F*, which he immediately dedicated to her. Friendship followed, and on 21 October Tchaikovsky wrote to Anatol:

I have become very friendly with Artôt and am glad to know something of her remarkable character. I have never met a kinder, a better, or a more clever woman.

By Christmas there was talk of a possible marriage and on 7 January 1869 Tchaikovsky consulted his father:

As rumours of my engagement will doubtless have reached you, and you may feel hurt at my silence upon the subject, I will tell you the whole story. I made the acquaintance of Artôt in the spring of this year, but only visited her once when I went to a supper given after her benefit performance. After she returned here in the autumn, I did not call on her for a whole month. Then we met by chance at a musical evening. She expressed surprise that I had not called, and I promised to do so — a promise I would not have kept (because of my shyness with new friends) had not Anton Rubinstein, in passing through Moscow, dragged me there. Afterwards, I received constant invitations and fell into the habit of visiting her house every day. Soon we began to experience a mutual glow of tenderness, and an understanding followed immediately. Naturally, the question of marriage arose at once and, if nothing hinders it, our wedding will take place in the summer . . .

My friends, especially Nikolay Rubinstein, are doing everything they can to prevent this happening. They declare that, married to a famous singer, I should play the pitiable part of 'husband of my wife', and that I should live at her expense accompanying her all over Europe . . .

If she will not give up the stage, I for my part would hesitate to sacrifice my future, for it is clear that I shall lose all opportunity of making my own way if I follow blindly in her train. You can see that my situation is a very difficult one. On the one hand I love her, heart and soul, and feel I cannot live without her any longer. On the other hand, calm reason bids me to consider more closely all the misfortunes with which my friends threaten me. I shall wait, my dear, for your views on the matter.

27

Mily Balakirev (1837-1910)

His father's reply was shrewdly equivocal, and did little to help solve the dilemma. But as it turned out Tchaikovsky was spared the decision for later in January, without so much as a word of warning, Artôt married a Spanish baritone in Warsaw.

Nikolay Rubinstein gleefully broke the news to Tchaikovsky during rehearsals for *The Voyevoda* which by this time had been resumed. Rubbing salt in the wound, he declared:

Wasn't I right when I told you she didn't need you as a husband! He's the right mate for her. But you — understand — you are needed by us, by Russia, and not as the servant of a famous foreigner!

Tchaikovsky turned pale as he listened to the gloating Rubinstein, and hurriedly left the theatre. His grief, however, was short-lived: it was his pride that had been wounded rather than his heart. He had mistaken infatuation for true love, and had confused Artôt the woman with Artôt the opera singer. A few days later he returned to rehearsals, apparently none the worse for his experience. He had, after all, escaped suffocation by a very powerful member of the opposite sex. Eight years later, he was not to be so fortunate.

The première of *The Voyevoda* was given at the Bolshoi Theatre on 11 February, 1869. The enthusiastic audience forced Tchaikovsky to take no fewer than fifteen curtain calls. Despite this initial success, interest in the opera soon evaporated, and it was withdrawn from the repertoire after only four further performances. Press criticism had been favourable with one very notable exception, that of Laroche. He attacked the opera for 'its lack of Russian temperament and abundance of German and Italian mannerisms.' These words deeply offended the composer and created a rift between the two men which lasted for a couple of years. In due course, however, Tchaikovsky came to accept the strictures of Laroche and destroyed most of the score, retaining only the overture, one chorus, an entr'acte and the dances which had proved so popular.

Two weeks after the première of the opera, Nikolay Rubinstein conducted the first performance of the symphonic poem *Fatum*. This, too, received a most enthusiastic welcome from the Moscow audience but in the end fared no better than *The Voyevoda*. After the Moscow concert, Tchaikovsky sent the score to Balakirev for performance in St. Petersburg, saying:

'I want to dedicate this work to you, but before doing so I should like to be assured that you do not find it utterly distasteful.'

Balakirev hastily made arrangements to conduct the work on 29 March, after which he replied to Tchaikovsky's letter:

House in Gaspal where Tchaikovsky worked on *The Voyevoda*

F.I. Schlijapin (1873-1938) in *The Voyevoda*

Scene from *The Voyevoda* in first performance at the Bolshoi Theatre in Moscow, 1869

Your *Fatum* has been played, and I venture to hope that the performance was not bad — at least, everyone seemed satisfied with it. There was not much applause, which I ascribe to the hideous crash at the end.

The work itself does not please me: it is not sufficiently thought out, and shows signs of being written hastily. In many places the joints and tacking-threads are all too clearly perceptible. Laroche says it is because you do not study the classics sufficiently, but I put it down to another cause: you are too little acquainted with modern music. You will never learn freedom of form from the classical composers. You will find nothing new there . . .

At the same concert, *Les Préludes* of Liszt was performed. Observe the wonderful form of this work — how one thing follows another quite naturally. This is no mere motley, haphazard affair. Or take Glinka's *Night in Madrid*: in what masterly fashion are the various sections of this overture fused together! It is just this organic coherence and connection which are lacking in *Fatum* . . .

I write to you quite frankly, and feel sure that you will not abandon your intention of dedicating *Fatum* to me. This dedication is very precious as indicating your regard for me, and on my part I reciprocate your feelings.

Tchaikovsky let the dedication stand although he refused to allow the work to be published. A few years later he destroyed the score, but after his death some orchestral parts were discovered and a reconstructed version was posthumously published as his Opus 77.

After the failure of *The Voyevoda* and *Fatum*, Tchaikovsky pinned his hopes on a new project which he had taken up in January. This was to be an opera based on a Russian translation of Fouquet's famous story *Undine*. By the end of the summer, which the composer spent at Kamenka, the score was finished and submitted to the Opera Directorate in St. Petersburg. The authorities prevaricated, and kept Tchaikovsky waiting for a decision until 1871, when the work was formally rejected. Two years later Tchaikovsky recovered the score and again consigned it to the flames, thus completing a trio of failures. He saved four pieces from the wreck: a wedding march, which later became the second movement of Symphony No.2; a love duet which became the famous adagio in *Swan Lake*, and the introduction of the work together with an aria which were later used as part of the incidental music to Ostrovsky's play *The Snow Maiden*. Tchaikovsky was not one to waste good material if it could be avoided.

Downcast by these three successive failures, Tchaikovsky once again became most uncertain about his future and returned to Moscow in a somewhat negative frame of mind. He soon found, however, another cause to champion — this time that of Balakirev, who in May had been forced to resign his position at the St. Petersburg Conservatoire by the Grand Duchess Elena Pavlovna, who strongly disapproved of the composer's musical tastes. Tchaikovsky regarded this as an unwarranted interference in the artistic affairs of the Conservatoire and, as he had done before in the case of Rimsky-Korsakov, published an article in the *Sovremennaya Letopis* attacking the Grand Duchess and stoutly defending Balakirev. Rimsky-Korsakov noted in his memoirs that the article 'impressed everyone very favourably by its warmth and forcefulness.' Certainly, it did much to reinforce the bond between Tchaikovsky and the nationalists, so much so that during the autumn of 1870 Tchaikovsky and Balakirev became constant companions. The friendship was still, however, not entirely without its reservations, for Tchaikovsky later confessed to Anatol that although he found Balakirev —

a very fine man and well disposed towards me, I still cannot get soul to soul with him. I do not like the narrowness of his musical opinions or the sharpness of his tone.

In fact, Tchaikovsky was more fortunate than he realised to be in the company of Balakirev at this particular time, for since his return from Kamenka he had complained bitterly of a dearth of musical ideas. His only composition had been a piano arrangement of the overture to Anton Rubinstein's opera *Ivan the Terrible*, for which he had been commissioned. But it was Balakirev who persuaded the composer to come out of his creative shell and to start work on a new and most important project.

Nikolay Rimsky-Korsakov, from the painting of V.A. Serov

Alexander Dargomizhsky (1813-1869), Russian composer

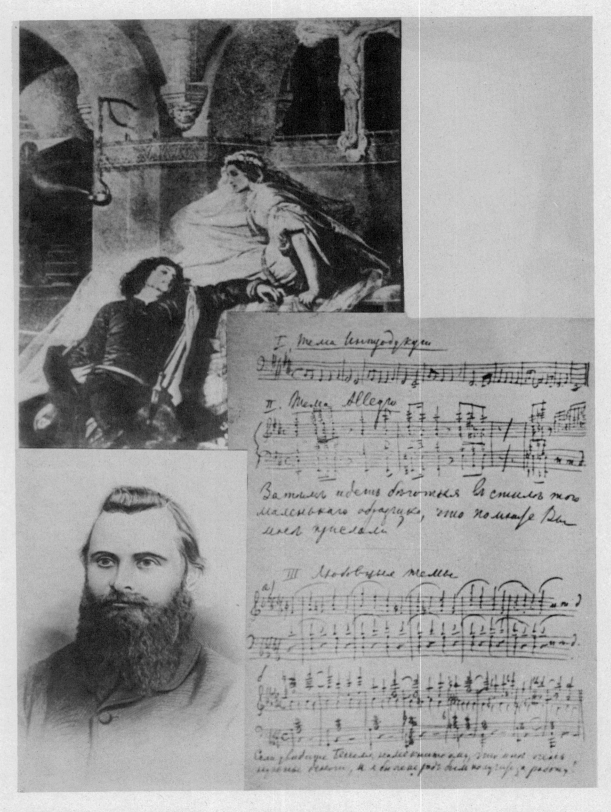

Illustration for Shakespeare's *Romeo and Juliet;* thematic material of the overture-fantasia "Romeo and Juliet" included in Tchaikovsky's letter to M.A. Balakirev; picture of Balakirev

Chapter 3

Towards Independence

'I must confess that I have but one interest in life; my success as a composer.' — Tchaikovsky

At Balakirev's insistence, towards the end of October Tchaikovsky started work on an overture to Shakespeare's *Romeo and Juliet*. The tragic tale of the 'pair of star-crossed lovers' fired his imagination and, early in November he was able to tell Balakirev that the work was progressing well. By the end of that month the score was complete and the parts were already being prepared for performance. Tchaikovsky sent the principal themes to Balakirev for his opinion, and at the same time asked him to accept the dedication. The reply he received was a lengthy criticism: the opening reminded Balakirev of a Haydn quartet, and although he found the love theme fascinating ('I often play it, and would like to hug you for it') he thought it lacked 'a mystic, inward, spiritual love'. But for all the work's shortcomings, he ended the letter by stating:

> I am impatient to receive the entire score, so that I may get a just impression of your clever overture, which is — so far — your best work; the fact that you have dedicated it to me gives me the greatest pleasure. It is the first of your compositions which contains so many beautiful things that I do not hesitate to pronounce it good as a whole.

Romeo and Juliet received its first performance at a Moscow Musical Society concert on 16 March 1870, conducted by Nikolay Rubinstein. According to Kashkin, the concert was a fiasco, due largely to Rubinstein's involvement in a court case the previous day which made him, rather than the music, the main object of the audience's curiosity. Rubinstein, however, was enthusiastic about the Overture, and set about arranging its publication by the German firm of Bote und Bock. Tchaikovsky revised the score throughout the summer and autumn of 1870, and in May 1871 *Romeo and Juliet* was published in its final form. Balakirev found the edition not entirely to his liking:

> It is a pity that you, or rather Rubinstein, should have rushed the publication of the overture. Although the new introduction is a decided

improvement, I still had a great desire to see some other alterations made, and hoped that it might remain in your hands somewhat longer for the sake of your future compositions.

Tchaikovsky, however, regarded the work as 'rather successful', although it was many years before it enjoyed great popularity. In *Romeo and Juliet* he had found a perfect subject, and had woven the ingredients of Shakespeare's tragedy into an abstract musical drama. In it, the fate of the lovers is his main concern, and he leaves the listener in no doubt that their tragedy was, in fact, their spiritual triumph.

Work during the latter part of 1869 had by no means been confined to *Romeo and Juliet*. Throughout November and December he composed his first set of songs, Op 6, which included the most famous he was ever to write *'None but the lonely heart'*. He had also been searching for a subject for a new opera and selected *Mandrago* to a libretto by Rachinsky who was a professor of botany. Only one chorus, completed in January 1870, was in fact written (*The Insect Chorus*), as he was dissuaded from continuing with the project by his friends, and in particular by Kashkin, who argued fiercely that the libretto 'gave too little scope for stage effects' and was more suited to a ballet than an opera'. Reluctantly Tchaikovsky accepted the advice and abandoned the idea. Instead, he turned to an historical novel *The Oprichnik* by Ivan Lazhechnikov. He began work in February and, from the outset, complained of slow progress. The disastrous première of *Romeo and Juliet* only made the situation worse: 'I just idle away the time cruelly and my opera *The Oprichnik* has come to a standstill at the first chorus'. Lack of progress was not the only reason for his depression: on 17 February he had written to his sister Alexandra:

One thing troubles me: there is no one in Moscow with whom I can enter into really intimate, familiar and homely relations. I often think how happy I should be if you, or someone like you, lived here. I have a great longing for children's voices, and for a share in all the trifling interests of a home — in a word for family life.

Two months later his mood was no brighter. He wrote to a friend that his nerves were 'all to pieces'; that his duties at the Conservatoire bored him to 'extinction', and that the slow progress of *The Oprichnik* was most probably 'due to the fact that no one takes any interest in what I write. I am very doubtful if I shall get it finished for at least two years'. It was small wonder that when news reached him that Vladimir Shilovsky was dangerously ill in Paris, he immediately set off to see him, stopping briefly in St. Petersburg where he learnt to his dismay that *Undine* had finally been rejected.

In Paris, Tchaikovsky found Shilovsky in better health than he

32

had expected, and within two weeks they moved on to Bad Soden, a German resort for consumptives, near Frankfurt. Bad Soden, with its depressing atmosphere, threw Tchaikovsky into deeper despair which was only relieved by a performance of Beethoven's *Missa Solemnis* in Mannheim ('one of the most inspired musical creations'), and a day spent at Wiesbaden in the company of Nikolay Rubinstein, whom he had discovered in 'the act of losing his last rouble at roulette . . . but convinced he would break the bank before he left!' The start of the Franco-Prussian war in July forced them to flee over the border into neutral Switzerland, where they remained for six weeks. Here, at last, Tchaikovsky was able to work on the revision to *Romeo and Juliet*.

On his return to Moscow in September, Tchaikovsky returned to the task of completing *The Oprichnik*, but found that progress was no better than before. He even considered abandoning the whole project and writing a four act ballet on *Cinderella* instead, but later changed his mind. The autumn of 1870 saw the completion of only three salon pieces — *Rèverie*, *Salon Polka* and *Salon Mazurka* Op 9, apart from the revisions to *Romeo and Juliet*.

The Davidov house at Kamenka — painting by Mihranyan

By the new year Tchaikovsky's financial position had become so critical that he was obliged to follow Nikolay Rubinstein's advice and stage a concert of his own works. An orchestral programme was out of the question due to the high costs involved, so he decided on a chamber concert for which he would compose a string quartet. Sensibly, Tchaikovsky realized that his name alone would not fill the hall of the Russian Society of Nobles which he had rented, and he therefore secured the services of Nikolay Rubinstein, Elizabeta Lavrovskaya, a young and popular singer with the Maryinsky Theatre, and the Quartet of the Russian Musical Society. The programme included 'None but the Lonely Heart', excerpts from The Voyevoda and the première of the String Quartet No 1 in D major, which Tchaikovsky had hurriedly written during February. This first all-Tchaikovsky concert took place on the evening of 28 March 1871 and was a huge success, made all the more prestigious by the presence of Russia's most renowned contemporary novelist, Ivan Turgenev, who was visiting Moscow at the time. The success of the concert gave Tchaikovsky a welcome boost to his morale. Laroche wrote of the occasion in glowing terms and considered the string quartet

distinguished by the same succulent melodies, beautifully and interestingly harmonised, the same nobility of tone — so foreign to the commonplace — the same slightly feminine softness, to which we have become accustomed in this gifted composer.

The excitement of the concert over, Tchaikovsky turned back to The Oprichnik, but he was now finding it increasingly difficult to work in Moscow. He complained to Alexandra:

I need great peace of mind to write satisfactorily, and I hardly ever attain it. Either I am at the Conservatoire, or I am seizing a free hour for composition in feverish haste, or someone wants me to go out, or I have visitors at home, or I am so tired out I can only fall asleep . . . I have already told you what an important part you play in my life, — although you do not live near me . . . This summer I will not fail to come to you.

With a feeling of immense relief, Tchaikovsky arrived in Kamenka during June where he spent most of the summer, enjoying the peace. Before returning to Moscow he visited a wealthy friend at Nizy, Nikolay Kondratyev, but soon the frantic social activity reminded him too much of Moscow, so he moved on to Ussovo and to Vladimir Shilovsky.

That peaceful summer of 1871 — peaceful at least so far as Tchaikovsky was concerned — convinced him that on his return to Moscow he must escape from the turmoil of the Rubinstein household and find quieter accommodation elsewhere. He therefore

View of Nice in 1875

rented a three-roomed flat which he modestly furnished within his limited means: a large sofa, a few cheap chairs and a portrait of Anton Rubinstein. He engaged a servant, one Mikhail Sofronov, whose brother in later years succeeded him and became Tchaikovsky's loyal companion. As Modest points out, it was in this way —

'that Tchaikovsky reached his thirty-second year before he began to lead an entirely independent existence.'

To augment his salary from the Conservatoire, he embarked on a brief, but revealing literary career as a music critic with the *Moscow Viedomost*. His reviews, though not of intrinsic literary value, are interesting for the light they shed on his musical opinions. For instance, he considered the Prelude to *Lohengrin* as 'perhaps the most successful, most inspired creation of the celebrated German composer'. Beethoven's 8th Symphony he thought to be one of his 'unsurpassable creations', while Chopin's E minor Concerto was 'unbearably long, senseless and hackneyed'. He was equally scathing about Schumann's 4th Symphony. Tchaikovsky's career as a critic lasted only until 1876 when he stopped writing reviews altogether.

The Oprichnik used up the rest of his free time during the autumn of 1871. He turned down a deluge of suggestions from Balakirev for other works. 'I dare say this unlucky opera will share the same fate as my *Undine* but all the same I want to finish it, so I can't begin another work just yet.' Work at the Conservatoire was becoming an increasing burden, and when, during the winter of 1871, it was

35

threatened with closure due to a lack of finances, Tchaikovsky admitted to Anatol that although he would be 'sorry and incensed if it falls apart', he would welcome the change as 'my work has become so distasteful to me'. To add to his misery, the opera continued to progress slowly. When, at the beginning of December, Shilovsky proposed a foreign trip, to the South of France and to Italy, Tchaikovsky jumped at the chance to escape from the oppressive atmosphere in Moscow: 'I must tell you', he wrote to Anatol on 14 December 'that at Shilovsky's urgent desire I am going abroad for a month. I shall start in about ten days' time, but no one —except Rubinstein — is to know anything about it: everyone is to think I have gone to see our sister'. His caution stemmed from a fear of the gossip which would most certainly have circulated had the truth been known: travelling in the company of a nineteen-year-old boy in the middle of the Season would hardly have been considered proper.

From Nice, Anatol received a letter remarking on the pleasure of the warm climate — 'one can walk without an overcoat' — but tinged with melancholy: 'I am old and can enjoy nothing more. I live on my memories and my hopes. But what is there to hope for?' After a month away he returned to Moscow. The only work accomplished during the trip were two piano pieces, both dedicated to Shilovsky: an F major Nocturne and the *Humoresque* in G minor.

During February and March 1872 Tchaikovsky resumed his labours over *The Oprichnik* and fulfilled a commission for a Festival Cantata to celebrate the 200th. anniversary of the birth of Peter the Great. By the end of May the opera was at last complete and in the hands of Eduard Napravnik (1839-1915), conductor of the St. Petersburg Opera and future champion of Tchaikovsky's music. It was not until the following November that the Opera Committee finally gave their approval. By this time Tchaikovsky was engrossed in his second Symphony, in C minor, for which he had made preliminary sketches during his summer sojourn at Kamenka. These had almost immediately been put aside as it was relaxation and not work that Tchaikovsky had wanted most. The Symphony was finished by the end of November, and from a letter he wrote to Modest on 14 November he appears to have been satisfied with the result:

'the symphony, which is nearing completion, occupies me so entirely that I can think of nothing else . . . It seems to me my best work, at least as regards correctness of form, a quality for which I have not so far distinguished myself.'

Tchaikovsky's satisfaction was intensified that Christmas when he was summoned to appear before the final selection committee of the

Tchaikovsky in 1873

Eduard Napravnik,
conductor and champion of
Tchaikovsky's music

Imperial Theatres in St. Petersburg. *The Oprichnik*
had been pronounced worthy of performance at the Maryinsky
Theatre. During his brief visit to the capital city he attended a party
at Rimsky-Korsakov's house, when he played through the Finale of
the new symphony. Later he told Modest that the whole party had
nearly 'torn him to pieces' so great had their enthusiasm been for a
work so solidly based on Russian folk-tunes. At the same party he
asked Stassov to suggest subjects for future orchestral work. The
critic recommended three: Shakespeare's *The Tempest,* Scott's
Ivanhoe or Gogol's *Taras Bulba.* For *The Tempest,* Stassov gave
Tchaikovsky a detailed programme and the composer decided that
this was to be his next major project.

On 7 February 1873 the Symphony No.2 in C minor (popularly
known as *Little Russian)* was premièred in Moscow under Nikolay
Rubinstein. The following day Tchaikovsky wrote to Stassov
describing its 'overwhelming success'. Laroche also gave the work a
glowing review: 'It is a long time since I have encountered a work
of art with so powerful a thematic development of ideas, such well
motivated and artistically worked-out contrasts'. Laroche's
enthusiasm, shared by the majority of critics, ensured the work's
future success and prompted a repeat performance on 7 March.
There was little doubt that Tchaikovsky was at last making his
mark.

37

Chapter 4

Travels and Solitude

'Fatalism engenders in every true Russian moments of gloom and depression such as we Westerners can little appreciate' — Edwin Evans

Further proof of Tchaikovsky's increasing importance and reputation came during March 1873, when the governing committee of the Moscow Imperial Theatres invited him to compose incidental music for a new play by Ostrovsky, *The Snow Maiden*. The score, consisting of nineteen items, was completed within three weeks and although the play itself only achieved a moderate success, Tchaikovsky's music immediately caught the public's attention and was published as his Opus 12. For this commission he received 250 roubles, which enabled him to make plans to spend the following summer abroad. The holiday turned out to be an eventful journey through Germany, Switzerland, Northern Italy and on to Paris. Of more importance to future music historians, however, is the fact that during his travels Tchaikovsky took up his earlier habit of keeping a diary. Modest assures us that:

every day had its great value for him, and the thought that he must bid eternal farewell to it and leave all trace of its experiences, depressed him exceedingly. It was a consolation to save something from the limbo of forgetfulness, so that in time to come he might recall to mind the events through which he had lived.

He had already destroyed the diaries of his childhood and his youth, considering their contents 'meaningless and ridiculous'. Later diaries would also be destroyed, but for very different reasons. His brother recalls elsewhere that Tchaikovsky began a new diary towards the end of the seventies, 'which he kept for about ten years. He never showed it to anyone, and I had to give him my word of honour to burn it after his death'. Modest kept his word, and with the help of other members of the Tchaikovsky family, he destroyed a number of diaries and letters in a vain attempt to sustain the elaborate cover-up concerning the composer's personal

life. What remains of the diaries makes fascinating reading. For instance, we learn that during the summer trip of 1873 it was clearly Tchaikovsky's intention to begin a new Symphony. The entry for 23 June reads:

Yesterday on the road from Vorushba to Kiev, music came singing and echoing through my head after a long interval of silence. A theme in embryo, in B major, took possession of my mind and almost led me on to attempt a symphony. Suddenly the thought came over me to cast aside Stassov's none too successful *Tempest*, and devote the summer to composing a symphony which would throw all my previous works into the shade.

He continues by quoting the theme, and even though a subsequent entry written 'not far from Dresden' goes on to quote an idea for the Introduction to 'the first allegro', no symphony was in fact composed that summer. By the beginning of August he was back in Russia, and staying at Vladimir Shilovsky's home in Ussovo.

Shilovsky had been called to Moscow unexpectedly, and it was not until five years later that Tchaikovsky described, in a letter to Mme. von Meck, the effect of the fortnight's solitude:

I was in a highly strung, emotional mood; wandered for whole days together in the forest, spent the evenings on the low-lying steppe, and at night, sitting at my open window, I listened to the solemn stillness which was only broken at rare intervals by some vague, indefinable sound. During this fortnight, without the least effort — just as though I were under the influence of some supernatural force — I sketched out the whole of *The Tempest* overture.

The Overture was orchestrated that autumn, despite the growing pressure of his teaching and reviewing duties. *The Oprichnik* was also a cause of concern, as still no date had been fixed for its première. During December he wrote to the publisher Bessel, who had been given the sole publication rights of the opera, that the directors of the Moscow Imperial Theatres had indicated their interest in mounting *The Oprichnik*. He went on to say that even though he had been assured by the *répétiteur* that 'no expense shall be spared in producing the opera brilliantly', he remained adamant that he would 'not consent to have the opera performed in Moscow unless it was produced in St Petersburg too!'. Bessell, acting on Tchaikovsky's behalf, eventually managed to resolve the problems towards the end of January 1874 when Tchaikovsky reluctantly agreed to several cuts demanded by the theatre authorities.

Meanwhile, *The Tempest* had been given its first performance on 19 December under Nikolay Rubinstein, and had met with much the same enthusiasm as the second Symphony. Throughout January 1874, Tchaikovsky worked on a new string quartet, which was first performed at a Soirée given by Nikolay Rubinstein. In his memoirs, Kashkin recalls the evening:

Early in 1874 the second String Quartet in F major was played at a musical evening at Nikolay Rubinstein's. I believe the host himself was not present, but his brother Anton was there. All the time the music was going on Rubinstein listened with a lowering, discontented expression, and at the end declared with his customary brutal frankness that it was not at all in the style of chamber music, that he himself could not understand the work, etc. The rest of the audience as well as the players, were charmed with it.

The first public performance of the Quartet was given on 22 March, and in spite of Rubinstein's hostility, was a remarkable success.

By this time rehearsals for *The Oprichnik* were underway at St. Petersburg and, at Napravnik's request, Tchaikovsky was present during April. Once more he was forced to agree to cuts and revisions and consequently began to hate the work. On 6 April he wrote to Albrecht that 'there is nothing really fine in the opera' and began advising his friends not to attend its première. His advice was ignored. On 24 April, Nikolay Rubinstein with almost the

The Grand Theatre of Moscow

Tchaikovsky in 1874

entire staff of the Moscow Conservatoire arrived at the Maryinsky Theatre, where they witnessed an outstanding success. At a dinner after the performance, Tchaikovsky was awarded the Kondratyev Prize of 300 roubles. Nevertheless, the opera received mixed reviews in the press. Predictably, Cui found 'the text . . . the work of a schoolboy' and the music 'equally unnatural and undeveloped . . . Tchaikovsky's creative talents, which are occasionally apparent in his symphonic works are completely lacking in *The Oprichnik*'. Laroche entirely disagreed: 'The wealth of musical beauties in *The Oprichnik* is so great that this opera takes a significant place not only among Tchaikovsky's own works, but among all the examples of Russian dramatic music.' The composer however accepted Cui's verdict and, in an attempt to escape further criticism in the press, left for Italy two days after the première. Thoroughly depressed, he visited Rome, Naples, Florence and Venice, but found no relief. On 2 May he wrote to Anatol:

today is the eighth day since I left Russia, and during the whole of this time I have not exchanged a friendly word with anyone. Except the hotel servant and railway officials, no human being has heard a word from my lips.

Rome from Mount
Aventino in 1875

From Naples on 9 May he wrote in an equally gloomy frame of mind to Modest:

You cannot imagine anyone who suffers more than I do . . . The main reason for all my misery is *The Oprichnik*.

In a later letter which refers to the opera tormenting him, he admits that

the opera is so bad I always ran away from rehearsals to avoid hearing another note . . . It has neither action, style, nor inspiration. I am sure it will not survive half-a-dozen performances.

Contrary to his pessimistic prediction, *The Oprichnik* received in all fourteen performances which, as Modest points out, 'was more than the average success when compared with other contemporary operas.' Abandoning his miserable stay in Italy, Tchaikovsky returned to Russia 'possessed by an intense desire to prove to himself and others that he was equal to better things than *The Oprichnik*'. By the middle of June, in Nizy, he was engrossed in work on yet another new opera.

A view of Naples in 1875

42

Alexander Serov (1820-71)

A few years earlier, the Grand Duchess Elena Pavlovna had commissioned a libretto, based on Gogol's story *Christmas Eve*, from the poet Yakov Polonsky. She originally intended it for Alexander Serov, who had been anxious to turn Gogol's story into an opera, but he had died in 1871 without starting work. In his memory, the Grand Duchess decided to offer a prize for the best setting of Polonsky's libretto, but when she too died, in 1873, the Russian Musical Society assumed responsibility for the competition, offering the winning entry, in addition to a cash prize, the guarantee of a performance at the Maryinsky Theatre. When Tchaikovsky heard of the competition and read the libretto he became fascinated. Gogol's amusing tale about Vakula the Blacksmith, who sells his soul to the devil in exchange for a pair of shoes for his lover 'as fine as the queen's', seemed the ideal antedote to *The Oprichnik*. His only reservation was that he felt he could no longer afford the time to write an opera unless he could be assured of its reaching the stage. After confirming that neither Balakirev, Anton Rubinstein nor Rimsky-Korsakov intended to participate, he felt confident of winning the competition. Within one month he completed his entry, which he called *Vakula the Smith*. But in his haste he had failed to realize that the closing date was one year ahead. When he discovered his mistake, instead of waiting patiently, Tchaikovsky launched into one of his less creditable campaigns: he lobbied Napravnik and the Grand Duke Constantine to stage his opera regardless of the other entries, and seized every opportunity of announcing publicly that he had entered the competition even though its first rule was for strict anonymity by all entrants. For this 'inconceivable degree of naïveté,' Tchaikovsky was severely reprimanded and was forced to write a lengthy apology to Napravnik admitting his 'stupid mistake', and assuring him that his intentions really had been honourable. In spite of this humble expression of regret, his devious attempts to win the competition did not cease, although for the moment he was content to let the matter rest. As a result his mood during the winter months of 1874 was one of constant irritability; his impatience to have *Vakula* produced and his dissatisfaction with the progress of his career threw him into a 'morbid frame of mind.' Even news from St. Petersburg of successful performances of the first String Quartet and *The Tempest* (which Stassov considered a 'marvel of marvels') failed to arouse his interest. Only when Laroche saw fit to publish a stinging criticism of *The Tempest* did Tchaikovsky react:

It is the general tone of his remarks that annoys me; the insinuation that I have borrowed everything from other composers and have nothing of my own.

43

The outstanding success of *The Oprichnik* in Kiev did, however, brighten his mood temporarily, and on 3 December he informed Anatol of the real reason for his moroseness:

I am now completely absorbed in the composition of a pianoforte concerto. I am very anxious that Rubinstein should play it at his concert. The work progresses very slowly, and does not turn out well. However, I stick to my intentions, and hammer pianoforte passages out of my brain: the result is nervous irritability.

His hopes for Nikolay Rubinstein's co-operation proved futile. On 21 January 1875, he complained in a further letter to Anatol that 'I am unable to shake off the effects of a cruel blow to my self-esteem.' Three years later he explained the cause of this 'cruel blow' in a letter to Madame von Meck:

To N. F. von Meck.

'San Remo, *January 21st (February 2nd),* 1878.

. . . In December, 1874, I had written a pianoforte concerto. As I am not a pianist, it was necessary to consult some virtuoso as to what might be ineffective, impracticable, and ungrateful in my technique. I needed a severe, but at the same time friendly, critic to point out in my work these external blemishes only. Without going into details, I must mention the fact that some inward voice warned me against the choice of Nicholas Rubinstein as a judge of the technical side of my composition. However, as he was not only the best pianist in Moscow, but also a first-rate all-round musician, and, knowing that he would be deeply offended if he heard I had taken my concerto to anyone else, I decided to ask him to hear the work and give me his opinion upon the solo parts. It was on Christmas Eve, 1874. We were invited to Albrecht's house, and, before we went, Nikolay Rubinstein proposed I should meet him in one of the class-rooms at the Conservatoire to go through the concerto. I arrived with my manuscript, and Rubinstein and Hubert soon appeared. The latter is a very worthy, clever man, but without the least self-assertion. Moreover, he is exceedingly garrulous, and needs a string of words to say 'yes' or 'no'. He is incapable of giving his opinion in any decisive form, and generally lets himself be pulled over to the strongest side. I must add, however, that this is not from cowardice, but merely from lack of character.

I played the first movement. Never a word, never a single remark. Do you know the awkward and ridiculous sensation of putting before a friend a meal which you have cooked yourself, which he eats — and holds his tongue? Oh, for a single word, for friendly abuse, for *anything* to break the silence! For God's sake say *something!* But Rubinstein never opened his lips. He was preparing his thunderbolt, and Hubert was waiting to see which way the wind would blow. I did not require a judgment of my work from the artistic side; simply from the technical point of view. Rubinstein's silence was eloquent. 'My dear friend,' he seemed to be saying to himself, 'how can I speak of the details, when the work itself goes entirely against the grain?' I gathered patience, and played the concerto straight through to the end. Still silence.

'Well?' I asked, and rose from the piano. Then a torrent broke from Rubinstein's lips. Gentle at first, gathering volume as it proceeded, and finally bursting into the fury of a Jupiter-Tonans. My concerto was worthless, absolutely unplayable; the passages so broken, so disconnected, so unskilfully written, that they could not even be improved; the work itself was bad, trivial, common; here and there I had stolen from other people; only one or two pages were worth anything; all the rest had better be destroyed, or entirely rewritten. 'For instance, *that?*' 'And what meaning is there in *this?*' Here the passages were caricatured on the piano. 'And look there! Is it possible that anyone could?' etc., etc., etc. But the chief thing I cannot reproduce: the *tone* in which all this was said. An independent witness of this scene must have concluded I was a talentless maniac, a scribbler with no notion of composing, who had ventured to lay his rubbish before a famous man. Hubert was quite overcome by my silence, and was surprised, no doubt, that a man who had already written so many works, and was professor of composition at the Conservatoire, could listen calmly and without contradiction to such an oration, such as one would hardly venture to address to a student before having gone through his work very carefully. Then he began to comment upon Rubinstein's criticism, and to agree with it, although he made some attempt to soften the harshness of his judgment. I was not only astounded, but deeply mortified, by the whole scene. I require friendly counsel and criticism; I shall always be glad of it, but there was no trace of friendliness in the whole proceedings. It was a censure delivered in such a form that it cut me to the quick. I left the room without a word and went upstairs. I could not have spoken for anger and agitation. Presently Rubinstein came to me and, seeing how upset I was, called me into another room. There he repeated that my concerto was impossible, pointed out many places where it needed to be completely revised, and said if I would suit the concerto to his requirements, he would bring it out at his concert. 'I shall not alter a single note,' I replied, 'I shall publish the work precisely as it stands.' This intention I actually carried out.

His immediate reaction was to obliterate Rubinstein's name from the title page of the manuscript and substitute that of Hans von Bülow (1830-94), a famous German pianist whom Tchaikovsky had heard in recital at the Bolshoi Theatre the previous March. Bülow, highly flattered by the dedication and already a champion of Tchaikovsky's music in Europe, regarded the Concerto as his 'most perfect work . . . the ideas are so lofty, strong and original . . . the form so perfect, mature and full of style.' He gave the first performance of the B flat minor Concerto in Boston during his American tour that October.

The confrontation with Rubinstein caused a serious breach in the friendship until the pianist finally relented in 1878. The whole episode threw Tchaikovsky into an acute depression that lasted until the autumn. In letters to the twins written during March, he

Hans von Bülow

complained of having been on 'the verge of despair' throughout the winter, and that he had often wished himself dead. During these months of despair, his only compositions were the *Sérénade Mélancolique* for violin and orchestra Op 26, and some songs (Opus Numbers 25, 27 and 28) all of which reflect the blackness of his mood. The future of *Vakula the Smith* still remained an obsession as this excerpt from a letter to Anatol reveals:

All my thoughts now are devoted to my beloved offspring *Vakula*. You cannot imagine how much I reckon upon this work. I think I shall go mad

46

if it fails to bring me luck. I do not want the prize — I despise it, although money is no bad thing — but I want my opera performed.

And he was still prepared to do anything to get *Vakula* staged. Already, Nikolay Rubinstein, one of the judges, had performed the Overture in Moscow. As though to make absolutely certain that the judges should be aware which was his entry, Tchaikovsky added a motto in his own hand-writing on the title page before submitting the corrected score.

Shortly before the summer holidays, this year to be divided between Ussovo, Nizy and Verbovka (an estate near Kamenka that also belonged to the Davidovs), Tchaikovsky received and accepted a commission from the Imperial Theatres for a ballet entitled *Swan Lake*, for which he would be paid a fee of 800 roubles. Although he confessed that the money was the main attraction of the project, he later said to Rimsky-Korsakov that 'I have long had a wish to try my hand at this kind of music'. The summer was spent working on a new symphony — No 3 in D major — which was finished by the middle of August, and the first two acts of *Swan Lake* which were completed by the time he returned to Moscow in September. From Rimsky-Korsakov he received a strong hint that *Vakula* had won the opera competition:

'I do not doubt for a moment that your opera will carry off the prize . . . except for your work I do not consider there is one fit to receive the prize, or to be performed in public.'

By the end of October, what everyone already knew was confirmed by the Grand Duke Constantine: *Vakula the Smith* had carried off the first prize.

Well pleased with himself, Tchaikovsky attended the première of the First Piano Concerto on 13 November in St. Petersburg. The pianist was an old school friend, Gustav Kross, and the conductor Napravnik. The reviews were almost all unfavourable, and the public's response no more encouraging. Laroche, while praising the Introduction, predicted that the work would have no future. Tchaikovsky himself, attributed the work's failure to the 'hopelessly mutilated' accompaniment of Napravnik. The Third Symphony received a more auspicious start under Nikolay Rubinstein on 19 November. Its success was immediate and Tchaikovsky considered the work 'a step forward' as regards form. Throughout the five movements there is little evidence of the melancholy from which Tchaikovsky was suffering at the time of its compostion. The symphony has since been nicknamed *The Polish*, apparently for no more valid reason than the *tempo di polacca* marking of the *Finale*. It is the most academic of

Tchaikovsky's symphonies, a fact which probably accounts for its present neglect. In striving after correctness of form — something which he always admitted was an impossibility for him — Tchaikovsky suppressed his natural style.

Two weeks later the B flat minor Concerto received its first favourable review after the Moscow première, with Taneyev (1856-1915) as soloist and Nikolay Rubinstein conducting. Tchaikovsky regarded his pupil's playing as having grasped completely his intention in all its most delicate and minute details. Alexander Famintoin gave a glowing review: 'it astounds the listener by its lucidity and joyousness of spirit from beginning to end'. To add to his pleasure, Tchaikovsky also received news from von Bülow in America that after every performance he had been obliged to repeat the entire Finale.

A major diversion during the autumn of 1875 was the visit to

A caricature of Camille
Saint-Saëns (1835-1921)

48

Tchaikovsky in 1875

Title page for *The Seasons,* twelve pieces for piano

Georges Bizet (1838-75)

Moscow of the French composer Camille Saint-Saëns (1835-1921), whom Tchaikovsky soon discovered to be a fascinating and witty companion. They soon realized a mutual ambition: to imitate the ballet-dancers they had so admired in their youth. As Modest soberly recalls:

This suggested the idea of dancing together, and they brought out a little ballet, *Pygmalion and Galatea* on the stage of the Conservatoire. Saint-Saëns, aged forty, played the part of Galatea most conscientiously, while Tchaikovsky, aged thirty-two appeared as Pygmalion. Nikolay Rubinstein formed the orchestra. Unfortunately, besides the three performers, no spectators witnessed this singular entertainment.

Despite these high jinks with the French composer, Tchaikovsky completed a cantata for the great Russian bass, Ossip Petrov, to celebrate his golden jubilee, and accepted a commission from the editor of *Nuvellist*, a musical magazine, to compose a series of twelve piano pieces which he intended to publish at the rate of one a month. Tchaikovsky came to regard this task as a chore, and relied on his servant to remind him the day before each publication date so that he could toss off a new piece in time to catch the press. The complete collection was in due course published (Opus 37b) and became popularly known as *The Seasons*.

Early in 1876 Tchaikovsky left Russia with Modest, who had accepted a post as tutor to a deaf and dumb boy, Nikolay Kondrati, and had to study in Lyons for one year as part of his training. The two brothers decided to go to Paris via Germany and Switzerland. Modest remembers his brother's delight at the innocence of his in-experienced travelling companion and his pleasure in acting as a guide 'to an unimpressionable tourist.' In Paris, they attended a performance of *Carmen* at the Opéra Comique at which, according to Modest, Tchaikovsky 'experienced one of the strongest musical impressions of his life'. Although he was no stranger to Bizet's music, for Shilovsky had sent him the piano version early the previous year, Modest claims that his love of *Carmen* now grew into 'an almost unwholesome passion'. It remained Tchaikovsky's favourite opera throughout his life.

On 22 January the brothers bade farewell to each other and Tchaikovsky returned home, the sketches of a new string quartet in his pocket. Two weeks later, on 6 February, he attended the St. Petersburg première of the Third Symphony, under Napravnik, which met with a cool reception, even though the composer himself was 'enthusiastically recalled'. Cui remarked that 'on the whole the new symphony shows talent, but we have a right to expect more from Tchaikovsky', a view to which Laroche was entirely opposed: 'this symphony is one of the most remarkable works produced during the last ten years'. Discouraged by the symphony's failure,

Ferdinand Laub

Richard Wagner (1813-83)

Tchaikovsky again began to doubt his own ability and his capacity to say anything new. Nevertheless, he continued work on the Third Quartet in E flat minor, and by 1 March the score was complete. It was dedicated to the memory of Ferdinand Laub, the first violinist of the Moscow Russian Musical Society quartet, who had died the previous year. This, the last quartet Tchaikovsky wrote, was well received at its first performance on 28 March in Moscow.

Throughout these months, work had also been steadily progressing on *Swan Lake* and by Easter, on 22 April, the score was finished. The strenuous efforts of recent months however, had taken their predictable toll of Tchaikovsky's health, and during May he was so unwell that his doctors advised him to take a water cure at Vichy. At the beginning of June he arrived in Kamenka, where his condition deteriorated to such an extent that he suffered 'terrible paroxysms of fear' and complained of a total lack of musical ideas. But by the end of the month he felt recovered enough to make his way to Vienna, where boredom became his chief symptom, and after meeting Modest and Kondrati, he reached Vichy where he stayed long enough for what Modest describes as a 'demi-cure'. Tchaikovsky's haste was due to an official engagement at Bayreuth: the first festival devoted entirely to Wagner's *Der Ring des Nibelungen*. His impressions of Bayreuth were published in several lengthy and colourful articles which appeared in *Russkiye Vyedomosti*. He sarcastically commented that 'throughout the whole duration of the festival, food forms the chief interest of the public; the artistic representations take a secondary place. Cutlets, baked potatoes and omelettes are discussed much more eagerly than Wagner's music'. At the same time he was pleasantly surprised to find that his reputation had already reached the German town — 'it appears I am by no means as unknown in Western Europe as I believed' — but even such a flattering discovery could not prevent him from disliking Bayreuth's 'uninterrupted bustle'. During his stay he made the acquaintance of Liszt, but Wagner himself failed to receive him — 'he no longer sees anyone'. As for Wagner's music, Tchaikovsky summed up his reaction in the following note:

'I brought away the impression that the Trilogy contains many passages of extraordinary beauty, especially symphonic beauty, which is remarkable, as Wagner has certainly no intention of writing an opera in the style of a symphony. I feel a respectful admiration for the immense talents of the composer and his wealth of technique, such as has never been heard before. And yet I have grave doubts as to the truth of Wagner's principles of opera. I will, however, continue the study of this music — the most complicated which has hitherto been composed.

Yet if the 'Ring' bores one in places, if much in it is at first incomprehensible and vague, if Wagner's harmonies are at times open to objection,

The Festival Theatre of
Bayreuth

as being too complicated and artificial, and his theories are false, even if
the results of his immense work should eventually fall into oblivion, and
the Bayreuth Theatre drop into an eternal slumber, yet the *Nibelungen
Ring* is an event of the greatest importance to the world, an epoch-making
work of art.'

Completely exhausted by his stay at Bayreuth, Tchaikovsky
returned home by way of Nuremberg and Vienna. On his arrival at
Kamenka he fell into the arms of his family and was deeply touched
by the warmth and intimacy of the Davidov household. The
poignant contrast between happy family life and his own solitary
condition proved too much for him, and in a pathetic attempt to
shape his own destiny he made an irrevocable and disastrous
decision.

He decided to marry.

Chapter 5

Anguish

'I am aware that my inclinations are the greatest obstacle to happiness; I must fight my nature with all my strength' — Tchaikovsky

Modest was the first member of Tchaikovsky's family to hear the alarming news when he received a brief note written from Verbovka on 31 August:

I have now to pass through a critical moment in my life. By-and-by I will write to you about it more fully, meanwhile I must just tell you that I *have decided to get married*. This is irrevocable.

Three weeks later, after he had returned to Moscow to begin the autumn term at the Conservatoire, Tchaikovsky kept his word and wrote to Modest in more detail:

I have been thinking much, these days, about myself and my future. The result of all these thoughts is that dating from today, I shall make a serious effort to marry, legally, anybody. I am aware that my inclinations are the greatest obstacle to happiness; I must fight my nature with all my strength . . . I shall do everything possible to marry this year, and if I am not brave enough for that, at any rate I shall conquer my old habits for once and all.

The most destructive part of Tchaikovsky's nature was at last ready to strike. His futile attempts to conquer his 'old habits' were to continue throughout his life, but during the autumn of 1876 he saw marriage as a convenient and ideal way of hiding them under a cloak of respectability. Even so, as a martyr meets his death, Tchaikovsky treated his impending submission to the ritual of marriage as the ultimate act of self-sacrifice. 'At this moment I hate, probably not less than you do, the beautiful, unknown being who will force me to change my way of living', he wrote to Modest at the end of September, and to Anatol he confessed that 'the quiet evening hours in my dear little home, the rest and solitude . . . have great charms for me. I shudder to think I must give it all up. And yet it will come to pass.' Then on 10 October, in the most revealing of his letters left in existence, Tchaikovsky wrote to Modest in these bitter, desperate, but very honest terms:

There are people who do not despise me for my vices only because they began loving me before they suspected I was a man with a lost reputation. Among them for instance is Alexandra. I know that she guesses everything and forgives everything. So it is with many of those I respect and care for most. Is it not a bitter thing to be pitied and forgiven when, truly, I am in no way guilty? So it has been a hundred times, and will be a hundred times more. In a word I should like to marry, or by some known liaison with a woman, shut the mouths of all despicable gossips, for whose opinion I do not care a bit, but who can hurt people close to me. Fulfilment of my plans is not as near as you think. I am so confirmed in my habits and tastes that to throw them away as one would an old glove is impossible. And then I have far from an iron will. Since my recent letters to you, I have already succumbed to my natural inclinations three times.

Marriage, of course, was to prove no answer to his problem. If anything, his foolish action calculated to 'shut the mouths of all despicable gossips' only served to swell their numbers and increase their malice. A few years later, in reply to a question from Nadezhda von Meck as to whether he had ever known non-platonic love, Tchaikovsky admitted that his was a hopeless case:

Yes and no. If this were put slightly differently, i.e. by asking if I have known complete happiness in love, the answer would be No, no and no!!! However, I think that it is in my music that the answer to your question lies. If you asked me if I have understood the whole power, the whole immeasurable strength of this feeling, the answer would be: Yes yes and yes, reiterating that I have passionately tried more than once to express in music the agony and at the same time the ecstasy of love. Whether I have succeeded in this, I do not know, or rather I leave for others to judge. I completely disagree with you that music cannot fully communicate one's feelings of love. I hold the complete contrary that only music can achieve this.

And it was to music during the autumn of 1878 that Tchaikovsky turned, as though to find relief from the path to self-destruction on which he was now so firmly set. On 6 October he completed the *Slavonic March* (popularly known by its French title as *Marche Slave*), a bombastic work employing Slavonic folk tunes and the Imperial Russian Anthem. He composed the piece for a benefit concert in aid of the victims of the Serbo-Turkish war, which had begun in June. Tsar Alexander II and his government supported Serbia in the hope that a Turkish defeat would enable Russia to regain much of the territory lost during the Crimean War. It was an error of judgement which cost the Tsar dearly. It was the Serbian army which was defeated, and Russia had little option but to

53

declare war on Turkey in 1877. During the winter months of 1876 the Russians were well aware that war was imminent, and the *Slavonic March* was Tchaikovsky's contribution to a wave of patriotism that was sweeping the nation. Under Nikolay Rubinstein, the March was greeted by a whole storm of patriotic enthusiasm at its première on 17 November. Even Cui was unstinting in his praise, considering it 'perhaps the most wonderful of all interpretations, in any artistic field, of the state of mind aroused by the event we have been witnessing.'

The *Slavonic March* was not the only work which occupied Tchaikovsky during that autumn. On the 26 October he completed a large-scale orchestral piece *Francesca da Rimini* which he claimed to have worked at 'con amore'. Even so, he failed to persuade Napravnik to include it in the programme of a forthcoming concert in place of some dances from *Vakula the Smith,* and *Francesca* was not heard publicly until the following year. By this time *Vakula* was in rehearsal at the Maryinsky Theatre for its opening on 6 December. Rehearsals had gone exceptionally well; singers and orchestra were unanimous in their praise. The production was well staged and Cui, for once, predicted a fantastic success. Tchaikovsky had every reason to feel confident that he had at last conquered the art form with which he had struggled for so long. He was bitterly disappointed. *Vakula* failed to stir the hearts of the opening night audience or the critics. To Taneyev, he later described the opera as a 'brilliant failure', and laid the blame entirely at his own feet: 'the opera is too full of unnecessary incident, and details, too heavily orchestrated and not sufficiently vocal'. And Cui eventually had to admit that the work 'lacked impact'. Almost simultaneously with *Vakula*'s failure, news arrived from Paris and Vienna that similar reactions had followed performances of *Romeo and Juliet.* In spite of these three setbacks in a row, Tchaikovsky was not depressed, and wrote a charming and individual tribute to his 'musical God' Mozart: this took the form of the *Rococo Variations* for cello and orchestra.

His ego received a well-needed boost the following month when Moscow was honoured by a visit from Leo Tolstoy. Tchaikovsky had been a great admirer of Tolstoy's works for many years, and regarded him as 'not so much an ordinary mortal as a demi-god'. In the great man's honour Nikolay Rubinstein took it upon himself to organise a musical evening at the Conservatoire, which included in the programme the *andante cantabile* from Tchaikovsky's first String Quartet. The composer wrote in his diary after the concert: 'Never in the whole course of my life did I feel so flattered, never so proud of my creative power, as when Leo Tolstoy, sitting by my side, listened to my *andante* while the tears streamed down his face.' Far less flattering was the reaction to his music for *Swan Lake*, during the rehearsals, which had begun early in 1877. The

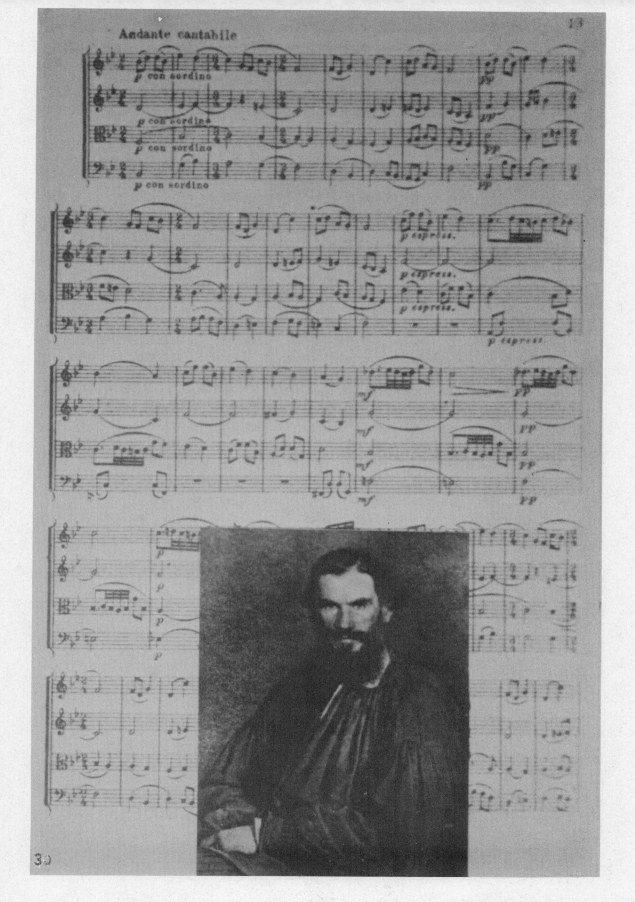

Andante cantabile from the first quartet

G. Ulanova in the role of Odette in *Swan Lake*

Leo Tolstoy

dancers complained that some of the score was 'undanceable', which made the Bolshoi authorities substitute music from other ballets. Of little more encouragement to Tchaikovsky was the general standard of the production; the sets and costumes were mostly second-hand and tatty, the choreography was by one Julius Reisinger, by all accounts a second-rater, and as if to complete the fiasco, the orchestra was conducted by a semi-amateur named Ryabar, who proved himself totally incapable of mastering what was left to Tchaikovsky's score. To the surprise of nobody, the première on 4 March was a dismal failure. The work was repeated a few times and then dropped from the repertoire. Of the critics only

55

An illustration of the second act of the disastrous first production of 'Swan Lake' at the Bolshoi Theatre 1877.

Laroche was enthusiastic, declaring it the finest ballet he had ever heard. It was not until after Tchaikovsky's death that interest in *Swan Lake* revived, and then it was due only to the efforts of one man, Marius Petipa (1819-1910) (choreographer of *The Sleeping Beauty*), that *Swan Lake* was eventually performed in its entirety on 27 January 1895. It then became clear that Tchaikovsky had at his first attempt, lifted the whole standard of Russian ballet by creating a masterpiece which has since influenced and inspired many other composers.

The difficulties over *Swan Lake* were to prove only minor irritations during 1877, the year in which Tchaikovsky came into contact with the two women who were to change his life so dramatically. The one he married brought him to the verge of suicide. The other became his saviour over the next thirteen years, and helped him to pick up the pieces of his life in the aftermath of the nightmare it was about to become.

Chapter 6

Disaster

'I can scarcely describe, Nadezhda Filaretovna, the spiritual tortures I underwent' — Tchaikovsky

During the month of December 1876, Tchaikovsky received a simple commission to make an arrangement for violin and piano. It came from Nadezhda Filaretovna von Meck, the wealthy forty-six year old widow of a famous engineer. He completed the task very quickly and on 30 December received a letter of thanks:

Gracious Sir, Peter Ilyich

Permit me to express my sincere gratitude for the speedy execution of my commission. To tell you into what ecstasies your work sent me would be unfitting, since you are accustomed to praise and admiration from those much better qualified than a creature so musically insignificant as I. It would only make you laugh; and my delight is so precious to me that I could not bear it to be ridiculed; so I shall content myself with asking you to believe absolutely that your music makes my life easier and more pleasant to live.

The following day she received his reply:

Gracious Lady, Nadezhda Filaretovna

Thank you most sincerely for the kind and flattering words that you have been good enough to write me. For my part, I can assure you that it is a great comfort for a musician, among all his failures and obstacles, to know of the existence of a few people, of whom you are one, who are true and passionate music lovers.

Madame von Meck was born Nadezhda Filaretovna, the daughter of middle-class parents, in 1831. From her father she inherited an intense love of music, and from her mother a business-like efficiency and force of character. Shortly before her seventeenth birthday she married Karl von Meck, son of a German Balt family and a lowly-paid engineer in government service. The first years of marriage were a constant struggle against poverty, which she found quite intolerable. But her intuition and her natural business instincts told her that there was money to be made in Russia, where

Nadezhda Filaretovna von
Meck

a vast railway building programme was launched in an attempt to
catch up with the progress already made by countries in Western
Europe. Her persuasive arguments and her confidence finally
convinced von Meck, and he relinquished his humiliating post in
order to set up in business on his own. The enterprise flourished,
and when he died in 1876 his widow inherited a considerable
fortune. She lived the life of a semi-recluse, running with her
customary efficiency a large mansion on the Rozdetvensky Boule-
vard with an army of servants, and seven of the twelve children of
the marriage.

She was genuinely upset by her husband's death: indeed, she had
good reason to be, as he had died of a heart attack on learning of her
infidelity. At the same time, she was glad to have escaped from both
the sexual demands of marriage and the rigours of child-bearing.
She later confessed to Tchaikovsky that she wished children could
be produced by artificial means. Thus, widowhood for her was a
release, and she returned to her first love, music, which gave her all
the emotional satisfaction she apparently required. One of her rare
visitors was Nikolay Rubinstein, who eagerly cultivated her

58

interest in the musical life of Moscow and especially that of the Conservatoire. She told him that she wished to engage, on a full-time basis, the services of a violinist whom she could accompany on the piano. Rubinstein immediately recommended one of his most promising pupils of the previous spring, whose name was Josef Kotek (1855-84). According to Modest, he was 'good-looking, big-hearted, enthusiastic and a talented virtuoso'. (Debussy was later engaged by her in a similar capacity.) Kotek had been a pupil in Tchaikovsky's theory class, and his admiration for the composer and for his music, had grown into devotion. Tchaikovsky in turn was charmed by Kotek's personality and musical talent, and the two men became close friends. The young violinist was delighted to discover that Madame von Meck shared his enthusiasm for Tchaikovsky's music, and not unnaturally he kept her very fully informed about his friend and his activities. It was in this way that she learned about the composer's financial difficulties and, as a result, commissioned him to make the violin and piano arrangement in December 1876.

Two months later Tchaikovsky received a second commission from her, which he duly completed. Her letter of thanks on this occasion put out a delicate feeler, inviting a more intimate friendship:

I should like to tell you a great deal more about my feelings towards you, but I am afraid of taking up your time, of which you have so little to spare.

Neither his financial position nor his temperament would allow Tchaikovsky to ignore an offer of this kind, and in reply he indicated that he regretted that she had not expressed her feelings and assured her that 'it would have been very pleasant and interesting, for I, too, reciprocate your feelings'. He invited her at some time in the future to write everything she wished to say.

Tchaikovsky in 1877

Nadezhda Filaretovna responded by writting a letter which ran to several pages. It was the first of over 1100 such letters during the next thirteen years. The correspondence was intimate — often passionate — and yet they were destined never to meet, apart from a few, brief and unintentional encounters. For each, their correspondence became a crucial support, a bastion against life and its misfortunes, and in their letters they developed a profound understanding and a deep mutual respect. Madame von Meck's lengthy reply to Tchaikovsky's cautious response in her letter of 19 March 1877, laid the foundation for the friendship which was to follow:

There was a time when I earnestly desired your personal acquaintance: but now I feel the more you fascinate me, the more I shrink from knowing you. It seems to me that I could not then talk to you as I do now . . . at

59

present I prefer to think of you at a distance and to be at one with you in your music.

She goes on to say that she was 'half-demented' after hearing Tchaikovsky's music for *The Tempest*:

I cannot tell you the impression it made on me . . . I took every opportunity of hearing what was said about you. Only a few days ago — in casual conversation — I heard one of your opinions, which delighted me and was so entirely in accordance with my own that I felt suddenly drawn to you by more intimate and friendly ties. It is not intercourse which draws people together so much as affinities of opinion, sentiment and sympathy, so that although one person might be united to another, in some respects they remain strangers.

It is clear that Tchaikovsky was delighted to accept Madame von Meck's friendship on the terms she offered: to him it must have seemed the ideal relationship 'which only a woman can give'. In his reply to her letter he agreed that they were of a 'kindred spirit', suffering from the same kind of misanthropy. Furthermore, he accepted without question her reasons for not wishing to meet him in person: 'I feel that on close acquaintance you would not find that harmony between myself and my music, of which you have dreamed.' He also assured her that he had followed her example and had taken steps to find out more about his new friend, and her way of life.

Madame von Meck offered Tchaikovsky a third commission in May 1877, in which she asked him to write for her an original piece, for violin and piano, to be called '*Reproach*'. Notwithstanding their rapidly-developing love affair on paper, the composer refused on the grounds that he 'could not bear any insincerity or falsehood to creep into our relationship' and that he was most reluctant to compose uninspired music for monetary gain. On the one hand he had come to realise that these commissions were badly-disguised charity: on the other, he would have preferred an outright loan as a much better way of paying off his debts. His letter continues:

At the moment I am absorbed in the symphony which I began during the winter. I should like to dedicate it to you, because I believe you would find in it an echo of your most intimate thoughts and emotions. Just now any other work would be a burden — work, that is to say, which would demand a certain mood and change of thought.

Nadezhda Filaretovna, delighted by the dedication and impressed by the composer's honesty, sent him by return post a loan of 3000 roubles.

The symphony to which Tchaikovsky referred was the Fourth, in F minor. Although this took up most of his available time, he was

Portion of the printed score for the Fourth Symphony, dedicated to N. von Meck, "my best friend"

Tchaikovsky in 1879

also seeking a suitable subject for yet another opera. One suggestion, by Stassov, he had already rejected: this was the offer of a libretto entitled *Cardinal*, based on Alfred de Vigny's *Cinq-Mars*. He wanted a subject 'dominated by a single dramatic motive, such as love (sexual or maternal), jealousy, ambition, patriotism, etc.' Another friend, Elizaveta Lavrovskaya, a singer, suggested Pushkin's *Eugene Onegin* as a possible theme, but Tchaikovsky rejected this idea as 'wild'. He was sufficiently intrigued, however, to return to Pushkin's text, and he was immediately enthralled by the plot and its musical potential. He spent a sleepless night sketching out a scenario, handing it to Konstantin Shilovsky the following day to enable him to work it out in more detail. Enthusiastically, Tchaikovsky wrote to Modest:

You have no idea how mad I am about this subject. How grateful I am to avoid banal Pharaohs, Ethiopian princesses, poisoned cups and all the rest of those tales written by automata. What poetry there is in *Onegin*!

I am not unaware of its faults. I know full well that it gives small scope for treatment and that it will be poor in stage effects. But the wealth of poetry, the human quality and the simplicity of the subject, expressed in Pushkin's inspired lines, will make up for what it lacks in other ways.

* * *

At the beginning of that eventful month of May 1877 Tchaikovsky received a letter quite out of the blue from Antonina Milyukova, one of his pupils at the Conservatoire. It was all the more surprising since it was a passionate declaration of love, which fell on extremely fertile ground. What actually went on in Tchaikovsky's mind is a matter for some speculation. Having set his sights firmly on matrimony, did he see this letter as yet another stroke of Fate? We know that he was completely under the spell of Pushkin's poetry and that he was 'hopelessly in love with the image of Tatiana', the tragic heroine of *Eugene Onegin*. Lost in the imaginary world of opera, did he confuse Antonina with Tatiana? It was certainly in his nature to do so, just as it was in his nature not to follow Onegin's example by rejecting this totally unexpected declaration of love. He was a bachelor, thirty-seven years of age, with a persistent and pathetic belief that marriage would 'shut the mouths of despicable gossips'. For whatever reason, he sent Antonina a reply in which, while he was careful to avoid any reciprocal declaration of love, he extended his gratitude and his sympathy. For Antonina, this was more than enough.

Antonina Milyukova was twenty years of age: she was unmarried, lived alone and was not particularly attractive. She was also a rather stupid person who believed that every man was madly in love with her. To her credit, it must be admitted that her moral character appeared to be entirely without blemish. As soon as she received Tchaikovsky's letter she invited him to call on her — an invitation which he accepted for reasons which he later described as totally inexplicable. There is a good deal of evidence to suggest that at this first meeting he did his best to explain to the infatuated woman why he was quite unable to reciprocate her feelings towards him, for in a letter dated 18 May she thanked him for his 'frankness'. But she was not to be deterred, for later in the letter she says:

Do not try to disillusion me about yourself, because you will only waste your time. I cannot live without you and so, perhaps, I shall soon put an end to my life. Let me look at you and kiss you so that I may carry that kiss into the next world.

Such a threat of suicide naturally appealed to Tchaikovsky's strong sense of drama, and he accepted it at its face value. During the weeks that followed he received further letters of a similarly pathetic nature, and found himself at the centre of a web of romantic intrigue. We learn from a later letter which he wrote to Madame von Meck that he found himself 'in a painful dilemma. Either I must keep my freedom at the expense of this woman's ruin . . . or I must marry.' Protesting that he would make a very unsatisfactory husband he proposed to Antonina early in June: she accepted him at once.

Tchaikovsky waited until 5 July before informing a member of his family of his engagement. Anatol received a disturbingly calm and lucid letter, describing Antonina as suitable in every way to be his future bride and 'possessed of one great attraction: she is as much in love with me as a cat'. He tells Anatol not to worry as he feels perfectly happy over the prospect of marrying, and adds, as if to prove his honesty, that 'I have been able to compose two-thirds of my opera'. The letter also included a brief note to his father, who 'jumped for joy' when he read the news.

Nadezhda von Meck did not hear of his future plans until 15 July, three days before the ceremony. Tchaikovsky's long letter is an attempt to justify his actions, but shows clear signs of panic:

Wish that I may not lose courage in the new life which lies before me. God knows I am filled with the best of intentions towards the future companion of my life, and if we are both unhappy I shall not be to blame. My conscience is clear. If I am marrying without love, it is because circumstances have left me no alternative. I gave way thoughtlessly to her first expressions of love; I ought never to have replied to them. But having once

Tchaikovsky and his bride

encouraged her affection by answering her letter and visiting her, I was bound to act as I have done. But, as I say, my conscience is clear: I have neither lied to her, nor deceived her, I told her what she could expect from me, and what she must not count on receiving.

Letters to Alexandra and Modest were not written until the day before the wedding, thereby ensuring that neither could protest.

On 18 July 1877, Antonina Milyukova became Antonina Tchaikovsky at St. George's Church on the Malaya Nikitskaya. Anatol and Kotek stood as the sole witnesses. That evening, the newly-weds left Moscow by train for a week's honeymoon in St. Petersburg. Tchaikovsky's 'terrifying, painful nightmare' had begun. Two days later he wrote Anatol the first of the agonising letters that were to persist over the next two months:

I should lie if I said I was happy . . . After such a terrible day as the eighteenth of July, after that ghastly spiritual torture, one cannot recover quickly . . . When the train started I was on the point of screaming, choked up with sobs. But I had to entertain my wife in conversation as far as Klin, to earn the right to lie in the dark in my own armchair, alone with myself. My only consolation was that my wife did not understand or realise my ill-concealed agony. She has looked quite happy and satisfied all along. *Elle n'est pas difficile.* She consents to everything and is satisfied with everything. We have had conversations that have made our mutual relationship clear . . . She needs only to fondle and take care of me.

He adds that once they have got used to each other 'she will not really bother me' because 'she is very limited . . . this is good. A clever woman would scare me. With this one I stand so high and dominate her to such an extent that I feel no fear of her'.

Tchaikovsky was making a courageous effort, but at the same time deceiving himself. Three days later he described her to Anatol as 'physically repulsive', and when the couple eventually returned to Moscow, Tchaikovsky was on the brink of mental and physical collapse. The only consolation he received was Nadezhda Filaretovna's courteous, but friendly letter offering congratulations on the marriage. Immediately he sat down and wrote her a desperate reply, pleading for a further loan of 1,000 roubles in order to escape: 'I need to go away, far away, to be alone, to rest, to think things over, to be treated, and lastly to work'. He was right to turn to Nadezhda von Meck for help: there he would receive a sympathetic hearing and he was well aware of the fact. She sent him the money by return post, advising him to go to the Caucasus without delay and to keep her informed of his progress. In a hastily-scribbled reply before he left, not for the Caucasus but for Kamenka, he wrote: 'If I emerge from this struggle victorious, it will be due to you and you alone'. He adds that he will write a full explanation from Kiev.

Two days later, on 9 August, he kept his word, and the letter Nadezhda Filaretovna received reveals the hysteria of a man on the verge of madness:

Nadezhda Filaretovna: here in brief, is a history of everything I have gone through since 18 July, the day of my marriage.

I wrote you that I was marrying without the urgings of affection because of circumstances I could not understand, circumstances that had placed me in a difficult dilemma. I had either to desert an honest girl whose love I had thoughtlessly encouraged, or to marry her. I took the latter course. In the beginning, I sincerely believed that I would fall in love with a girl so truly devoted to me. Also, I realized that my marriage was realizing the dreams of my aged father and other dear ones. The moment the wedding was over, and I found myself alone with my wife and realized that our future lot was to be inseparably united, I suddenly realized that I did not feel even ordinarily friendly towards her, but that I abhorred her in the fullest sense. I became certain that I — or, rather, music — the finest and perhaps the only fine part of my being — had died for ever. The future appeared to me the merest vegetable existence, a sordid comedy not to be endured.

My wife is not guilty at all. She did not ask me to marry her. It would, therefore, be cruel and spiteful of me to make her understand that I dislike her and look upon her as an unbearable nuisance. All I can do is act a part. But to act a whole lifetime is unbearable. How could I ever work? I was in despair, particularly as no one was near to whom I could turn for support and encouragement. I wished fiercely for death. Death seemed the only way out, but suicide was out of the question. I love some members of my family — my sister, my two youngest brothers, and my father. If I decided on suicide and committed it, I should be killing them. And there are many others, loved friends whose affection binds me to life. And I have the frailty — if it can be called one — to love life, love my work, love the prospect of success. I have not yet said everything I have to say, all I want to utter before the hour of my migration to oblivion. Death does not come to me. I shall not, and cannot, go to death. What is left?

I have told my wife that I shall travel for my health during August, as I am really unwell and need strict treatment. As soon as I had told her that, my journey began to seem like an escape from prison, however temporary. I found the strength to endure in the thought that the day of my departure was close. We were in Petersburg one week and then came back to Moscow. There we found ourselves without money, as one Kudryavsev had duped her when he had made her believe he would sell her forest land. A new series of tortures and anguishes set in: uncomfortable quarters, the need to arrange a new home, inability to do so without funds, all possibility of getting away removed by the same lack, worry, and a life of stupid idleness in Moscow (I had no impulse to work, and our quarters were highly uncomfortable), no friends, not a moment's respite from it all. I do not understand how I remained sane.

Then I had to visit my mother-in-law. There my torments multiplied. I detest the mother and the whole membership of the family I have entered. They have narrow ideas and freakish opinions and are constantly quarrelling. My wife (this may be unfair) became more abhorrent to me each hour. I can scarcely describe, Nadezhda Filaretovna, the spiritual tortures I underwent. Before leaving for the country, in one desperate attempt to get out of the terrible situation, longing to get away, I turned to someone you know well, a sweet and loved friend living at Braïlov. The idea that she would help me, the assurance that she would liberate me from these terrible chains of grief and madness, supported me. But would my letter get to her? Fear that my letter might go astray was torturing me. We went back to Moscow.

That awful life dragged along for several days. I had two distractions: first, a good deal of wine, which made me dizzy and gave me some minutes of forgetfulness, and, second, cheering talks with Kotek. He is the only one besides yourself who knows all that I am writing you now. He is good in the true sense of the word. That sorrows do not come singly is a fact. I received word of the sudden death of one of my closest friends, Adamov. We were in school together, started our service together, and despite our paths having parted, remained close friends until he died. He had every good fortune in life: flawless health, an excellent official position, money in his wife's name, an utterly happy family life, then, suddenly, death. It quite unnerved me.

Finally, one blessed evening, there was a letter from Braïlov. I began to cheer up a little. The remaining days were taken up by preparations for leaving and arrangements for future quarters, and on Tuesday at 1 p.m. I left. I don't know what I'll do next, but I feel as though I had awakened from a terrifying, painful nightmare, or, better, from a protracted illness. Like a man convalescing from fever, I remain very weak. I think consecutively only with difficulty. Even writing this letter has been a struggle. But what a sensation of sweet rest, and what an intoxicating sense of freedom and solitude!

If I understand my make-up correctly, it is altogether possible that when I have rested and quieted my nerves, I shall be able to return to Moscow and my customary routine, and regard my wife in a different light. In truth she has many qualities that can contribute to my future happiness. She likes me sincerely, and desires nothing more than my peace and happiness. I pity her.

I shall remain in Kiev one day. To-morrow I go to my sister, and thence to the Caucasus. Forgive the incoherence and jumpiness of this letter, Nadezhda Filaretovna. My nerves and my entire spirit are so weary that I can scarcely bring two thoughts together. However fatigued my spirit is, it is not so broken that it cannot warm with unlimited, profound gratitude to the hundred-times-priceless friend who is saving me. Nadezhda Filaretovna, if God gives me the strength to get through the terrible present, I shall prove to you that this friend has not helped me in vain. I have not written one tenth of what I want to say. My heart is full. It wants to pour itself out in music. Who knows? It may be that I shall leave behind something really worthy of renown of an artist of the first category! I have the daring to hope so. Nadezhda Filaretovna, I bless you for everything you have done for me. Farewell, my best, my most loved sweet friend.

His retreat to the warmth and security of Kamenka had a soothing effect on Tchaikovsky's shattered nerves, although he found work quite impossible during the early part of his stay. By 23 August however, he had recovered sufficiently to start orchestrating his new, fourth symphony, and sent regular progress reports to Nadezhda Filaretovna. She, in turn, responded with kind and sympathetic words. Thus encouraged, Tchaikovsky described the music to her and explained that although the first movement was 'very long and complicated' he regarded it as the best. He placed particular emphasis on the *pizzicato* effect used in the Scherzo and expressed the hope that the innovation would prove successful in performance. By 11 September he reported that he was also working on the orchestration of the first scene of *Eugene Onegin*. It is

Alexander Pushkin

clear that by this time his initial enthusiasm for the opera had
subsided and that he now felt that it was destined to fail. Nevertheless, he still cherished the hope that it would appeal to 'those
capable of seeking in an opera a musical re-creation of everyday,
simple emotions, common to all humanity and far removed from
tragedy and theatrical effect'.

As the time came for him to leave his beloved Kamenka and to
face up to the reality of the situation which awaited him in
Moscow, his nervous symptoms inevitably started to reappear. In a
letter to Anatol he expressed complete indifference to his wife and
to the prospect of seeing her again, although he did add — by way
of consolation either to himself or to Anatol — that 'she does not
scare me: she is simply an annoyance.' When he arrived in Moscow
on 23 September, Antonina was at the station to meet him and together they returned to the apartment she had so carefully prepared
for him. By the following morning his sense of utter desperation
had returned: already the apartment on which his wife had lavished
so much care had become a prison and, as he confessed to Anatol,
he felt extremely frightened. In a letter to Madame von Meck, who
at that time was on holiday in Italy, he expressed a single wish that
he would be given 'a chance to run away somewhere. But how, and
where? It is impossible, impossible, impossible!'

When Tchaikovsky resumed his classes at the Conservatoire, Kashkin recalls that he was obviously in an extremely nervous state although he did his best to appear quite relaxed. At a dinner party given by the Jurgensons, he appeared in public for the first time with his new bride. At first she created a 'generally favourable impression', but by the end of the evening the party had become 'rather colourless' due largely to the fact that Antonina was quite unable to make conversation, even on trivial subjects, without the assistance of her husband. Most of his friends and colleagues were unaware of the extent of Tchaikovsky's agony as he edged nearer to the brink of madness, and lost all capacity to assess the situation in which he had placed himself, in a rational manner. On one occasion, during the early part of October he waded, fully-clothed, up to his waist in the freezing, ice-covered waters of Moskva River in the hope that he would catch pneumonia and die. Panic seized him when he realised that his robust physique would withstand this suicide attempt and, in desperation, he telegraphed Anatol on 5 October demanding that he wire back immediately, in Napravnik's name, requesting his urgent presence in St. Petersburg. Anatol fell in with the subterfuge, and after a hasty explanation to his colleagues at the Conservatoire, Tchaikovsky took himself off to the capital. Modest records that the composer was 'scarcely recognisable' when his brother Anatol met him at the railway station for 'his face had entirely changed during the course of a single month'. As soon as he reached his hotel, Tchaikovsky suffered a complete nervous collapse, after which he remained unconscious for two days. The loyal Anatol never divulged the full details of what precisely took place on that occasion, but we do know that the doctor who attended Tchaikovsky prescribed, as the only possible cure, 'a complete change of life and scene'.

Anatol himself, now thoroughly alarmed by his brother's condition, left him as soon as it was safe to do so, in order to consult Nikolay Rubinstein. It was agreed that Antonina must be advised that divorce was a vital necessity. However, Rubinstein feared that Anatol would not be strong enough to handle the situation by himself and he insisted on accompanying him to Moscow, where they were courteously received by Tchaikovsky's wife. Rubinstein came directly and bluntly to the point as tea was being offered to the visitors, and to their great astonishment Antonina at once consented to a divorce, without making difficulties of any kind. Their mission having been accomplished with such surprising ease the two men prepared to take their leave, and as they did so Anatol was quite stunned to realise that the only thought in Antonina's mind was her delight at having entertained to tea so distinguished a celebrity as Nikolay Rubinstein. Neither her husband's condition nor the break-up of the marriage appeared to be of any consequence to her. What Anatol quite failed to discern was that Antonina's unnatural calm was, in truth, an early sign of her own impending mental illness.

With the separation now formally arranged, Tchaikovsky's health improved and on 13 October he was able to tell Modest that he was 'returning to life'. Antonina, however, was less fortunate. Alexandra took pity on her sister-in-law and gave her shelter for a time, but she quickly found Antonina's fits of weeping unbearable, not to mention the way in which she bit her nails to such an extent that spots of blood were scattered throughout the house. Eventually she had to order Anatol to take the stricken woman away from Kamenka.

During the years which followed, Antonina wrote many threatening letters to Tchaikovsky and to members of his family, having renounced her earlier agreement to grant him a divorce. She consoled herself with many lovers, and produced a large number of children as a result. In 1896 she was finally certified as insane. She spent the rest of her life in an asylum, where she died in that year of bloodshed and revolt which marked the end of Imperial Russia — 1917. To say that hers was a marriage doomed from the outset is an understatement. The brutal fact is that of all the women Tchaikovsky might have chosen as his wife, none was less suited or less equipped to fulfil that rôle than poor Antonina Milyukova.

Chapter 7

Escape to the South

'All I have done so far seems to me poor and imperfect compared with what I *can, must* and *will* do in the future.' — Tchaikovsky

Tchaikovsky made a remarkably swift recovery from his complete nervous collapse for within a week of regaining consciousness he was in Berlin with his brother Anatol, en route for Switzerland. From Berlin he wrote his publisher Jurgenson seeking commissions for 'songs, compositions, translations' — anything, in fact, to keep him occupied until he felt strong enough to resume work on his Fourth symphony and *Eugene Onegin*. On 20 October the brothers arrived at Clarens where they rented a villa standing on the shores of Lake Geneva — the Villa Richelieu. Having dealt with the problem of Antonina, or at least having escaped from it, his main concern was his precarious financial position once again. Modest recalls that his brother had 'only money enough to last five or six weeks'. As soon as they were comfortably installed in their lakeside villa, Tchaikovsky wrote a long letter to Madame von Meck in Moscow in which he described the 'unbearable mental agonies' of recent weeks and expressed his immense relief on having escaped 'the whirlpool of lies, pretence and hypocrisy'. With these preliminaries out of the way, he then addressed himself to the main purpose of his letter:

Now, I find myself in the midst of beautiful countryside, but in a most dire mental state. What will happen next? I cannot return to Moscow. I cannot see anyone. I am afraid of everyone. Finally, I am idle and unfit for work . . .

I must stay here for a time, rest, and let the world forget me. I must arrange for my wife's comfort and think over my future relations with her . . .

I need money again, and again I can ask no one but you. It is terrible, it is painful and lamentable but I must do it, must again rely on your infinite kindness . . . Oh, my sweet friend, in the midst of my tortures in Moscow, when I thought there was no way out but death, when I gave way to total despair, there were times when I thought only you could save me. And when my brother came abroad with me I realised that I could not exist

View of Lake Geneva with
Mont Blanc in the distance

without your help, and that again you would come forward as my saviour
. . . I still feel that you are my friend, a friend that can read my very soul in
spite of the fact that we know each other only by letters.

Ironically enough, when Tchaikovsky wrote this letter on 23
October help was already on its way. The generous Nadezhda
Filaretovna, having learned of Tchaikovsky's plight from the
ubiquitous Nikolay Rubinstein, immediately despatched the sum of
6000 roubles to Clarens, the first of such annual allowances which
she made to Tchaikovsky during the next thirteen years. As a
result, his way of life changed dramatically and, in Modest's words,
he became 'an independent man as regards his material welfare, and
a new life opened out before him . . . he had attained that freedom
of existence which was indispensable to his creative activity.'
In this way, Tchaikovsky was very quickly released from both
matrimonial and financial burdens: to a cynical observer it would
seem that his attempted suicide in Moscow, and his flight from
reality in St. Petersburg, had paid handsome dividends. Perhaps
not surprisingly he at once found Switzerland a sympathetic place
in which to work, and by 1 November both his recovery and the
first act of *Eugene Onegin* were complete. But good fortune, when it
comes, does nothing by halves, and on that same day he learned

71

that the directors of the Russian Musical Society in Moscow, at Nikolay Rubinstein's suggestion, had voted to pay him the balance of his salary in recognition of his 'enormous services' to both the Society and to the Conservatoire. This news came with a sympathetic note from Rubinstein advising the composer to calm himself and to 'take care of your health and to fear nothing. You are too highly valued as a musician to be compromised by secondary considerations.' In a grateful reply, Tchaikovsky told Rubinstein that the first scene of his new opera would soon be on its way to Moscow, and that he would like nothing more than to have the work performed at the Conservatoire.

Rubinstein's determination to help Tchaikovsky, and the effective way in which he set about things, were quite remarkable. As well as alerting Madame von Meck and persuading the Russian Musical Society to pay his full salary despite his sudden departure from Moscow, Nikolay Rubinstein was also instrumental in securing for the composer an official invitation to become Russia's delegate to the Paris Exhibition of 1878 — an appointment that carried a salary. Tchaikovsky had considerable doubts about his fitness for the post, and inadvertently left the invitation unanswered.

Meanwhile, Madame von Meck had sent a reply to Tchaikovsky's begging letter on 29 October. This reached him a few days later:

Now I know everything that has happened, my poor friend, it makes my heart ache to think of your suffering and of how your life has been spoiled. Yet I am glad that you have taken a definite step — it was necessary, the only thing to do. I did not let myself tell you before what I truly thought, because it would have seemed gratuitous advice, but now I believe I have the right, as a person so close to you in spirit, to give you my real opinion. And I repeat, I am glad that you escaped from the hypocrisy and lies — not for you, these things, and not worthy of you. You tried your best for another's sake, you fought to the end of your strength, certainly without profit to yourself; a man like you can perish in such circumstances, but he can never reconcile himself to them.

She continued by reproaching him for being ashamed of asking for her help:

Are we really such strangers? Do you not realize how much I care for you, how I wish you well in everything? In my opinion it is not the tie of sex or kindred which gives these rights, but the sense of mental and spiritual communion. You know how many happy moments you have given me, how grateful I am, how indispensable you are to me, and how necessary it is that you should remain just as you were created; consequently what I do is not done for your sake, but for my own. Why should you spoil my pleasure in taking care of you, and make me feel that I am not very much to you after all? You hurt me. If I wanted something from you, of course you would give it me — is it not so? Very well, then we are quits. Do not interfere with my management of your domestic economy, Peter Ilyich.

Any doubts that she may have had about the extent of his friendship were immediately dispelled by his reply written from Clarens on 6 November. He was to give her the thing she most desired: his music.

I thank you for everything, my invaluable friend. I do not suppose that I shall ever have an opportunity of proving that I am ready to make any sacrifice for you in return . . . therefore I can only please and serve you by means of my music. Every note which comes from my pen in future will be dedicated to you. To you I owe this reawakened love of work, and I will never forget for a moment that you have made it possible to carry on my career. Much, much, still remains for me to do. Without false modesty, I may tell you that all I have done so far seems to me poor and imperfect compared with what I *can, must* and *will* do in the future . . .

I am continually haunted by the thought of a long visit to Italy, so I have decided to start for Rome in about a fortnight. Afterwards we shall go to Naples or Sorrento . . .

Gradually I am going back to my work, and I can now definitely say that *our* symphony will be finished by December at the latest . . . May this music, which is so closely bound up with the thought of you, speak to you and tell you that I love you with all my heart and soul, my best incomparable friend.

During this exchange of letters Nadezhda Filaretovna's feminine curiosity got the better of her and she asked Tchaikovsky to send her a full description of Antonina Milyukova. Tchaikovsky readily obliged by accusing his wife of having an empty heart as well as an empty head and, even worse, of not knowing a single note of his music. He does concede, however, that she acted with honesty and sincerity throughout the whole miserable affair. Madame von Meck granted him full absolution in her reply:

You are not guilty of wronging her in any way, and you may be sure she will not suffer at all from the separation. (Antonina) is one of those fortunate ones who, because they lack education, never suffer deeply or for long since they cannot feel anything deeply . . . If someone tells you that she weeps, do not be disturbed: be sure she does it only for show.

These words were precisely what Tchaikovsky wanted and needed to read. There is more than a hint of self-satisfaction in her letter, but Madame von Meck waited two years before she revealed her true feelings about Tchaikovsky's marriage. In the meantime she was quite content to allow the correspondence to dwell on less intimate matters, and entered a long and rambling discussion on religion and on philosophy, prompted by Tchaikovsky's statement that a 'divine Providence' had led him on. He admitted having a 'dual temperament'. He refused absolutely to accept 'the dogmatic teaching' of the Russian Orthodox or any other established Church. At the same time he enjoyed the 'poetical charm' of the liturgy and, despite his lack of conviction, found himself 'calling upon God in grief, and thanking Him in his happiness'. Although he claimed to have found no solution to his 'contradictions', he was quite certain of one thing — 'that there is no personal or individual immortality'. In this context he examines the nature of music:

> I have reached a very mature age without resting upon anything positive, without having calmed my restless spirit either by religion or philosophy. Undoubtedly I should have gone mad but for *music*. Music is indeed the most beautiful of all Heaven's gifts to humanity wandering in the darkness. Alone it calms, enlightens and stills our souls. It is not the straw to which the drowning man clings; but a true friend, refuge and comforter, for whose sake life is worth living. Perhaps there will be no music in Heaven. Well, let us give our mortal life to it as long as it lasts.

* * *

During November the brothers visited Italy, an experience which Tchaikovsky found depressing, although he did manage to

St. Mark's Square, Venice

74

Tchaikovsky's faithful
servant Alexey Sofronov
and his wife

complete the orchestration of the whole of the first act of *Eugene Onegin* during their stay in Venice. It was at this point that Anatol received the letter from the Davidovs which, in effect, ordered him to return home at once and remove Antonina from Kamenka. Tchaikovsky travelled with his brother as far as the Hapsburg capital, Vienna, partly to bid him farewell, and partly to meet his servant, Alexey Sofronov, who had been summoned from Moscow as a replacement for Anatol.

Meanwhile, the lengthy correspondence with Madame von Meck continued unchecked. On 8 December he wrote to her from Vienna saying that he had found a performance of Wagner's *Die Walkürie* 'wearisome' — 'not a single broad, rounded melody', and that Brahms's First Symphony left him equally unmoved: 'He has no charms for me. I find him cold and obscure — full of pretensions but without any real depth.' In sharp contrast, we find that music by French composers aroused his warm enthusiasm: after hearing the *Sylvia* ballet music by Delibes he told Madame von Meck that his own *Swan Lake* 'was poor stuff by comparison.' He went on to say that during the past few years nothing had charmed him as much as the Delibes score apart, of course, from his beloved *Carmen*.

Having despatched his brother and collected his manservant, Tchaikovsky left Vienna and returned to Venice for a brief stay, during which time he took up once again the manuscript of the neglected Fourth Symphony. On 15 December he found time to express some displeasure at a parallel which Madam von Meck had drawn between music and alcoholic intoxication:

A man has recourse to wine in order to stupefy himself and produce an illusion of well-being and happiness. But this dream costs him very dear . . . wine can only bring a momentary oblivion to all our troubles — no more . . . Music is no illusion, but rather a revelation.

It was a case of protesting too much, for very shortly afterwards, in a letter to Anatol, he freely confessed that he was drinking rather a lot — a habit which persisted throughout his lifetime:

I cannot do without it. I never feel calm except when I have taken a little too much. I have accustomed myself so much to this secret tippling, that I feel a blind joy at the sight of the bottle I keep near me.

Early in January 1878 he arrived at San Remo, where he had arranged to spend a holiday with Modest and Kondrati. He was horrified to find waiting for him a letter from the Director of Finance at the Conservatoire which confirmed his salary of 1000 roubles as Russian delegate to the Paris Exhibition. He had forgotten all about this offer, and the authorities had taken his silence as acceptance. In panic, Tchaikovsky replied saying that he was unable to take up the post on account of ill-health. Nikolay Rubinstein, who had done so much to secure the appointment for his friend, was furious, and accused Tchaikovsky of feigning illness in order to escape his commitment. In reply, Tchaikovsky assured him that his presence in Paris would not further the cause of Russian music, and in reply to the charge of malingering, he said: 'How little you know me . . . Possibly you are right, and I am *putting it on* . . . but that is the very nature of my illness.' How Rubinstein reacted to this piece of elementary casuistry we do not know, but Tchaikovsky remained adamant in his refusal to go to Paris.

Tchaikovsky with Kondradi and Argutinsky

Scene of Paris, about 1891

Front and back of a 100-rouble note

Despite this contretemps, San Remo worked its magic on the composer and by 7 January the Fourth Symphony was complete. Three days later the score was on its way to Moscow, with a dedication on the title page which read, 'To my best friend'. Rubinstein kept silent until after the symphony had received its first performance on 22 February. Even at that point, he merely informed Tchaikovsky that the work had been performed, without giving the slightest indication as to his own opinion of the symphony or the manner in which it had been received by the public. Frustrated by this silence from Moscow, the composer was delighted when he received both a telegram and a letter from Madame von Meck expressing her delight at the new symphony, and describing the première as successful, despite the inadequate playing of the orchestra. She asked if there was a programme to the work, and although Tchaikovsky often denied that his symphonies were in any way programmatic, he set out one in full and colourful detail for 'his best friend':

What joy your letter brought me today, dearest Nadezhda Filaretovna! I am inexpressibly delighted that the symphony pleases you: that, hearing it,

San Remo about 1877

77

you felt just as I did while writing it, and that my music found its way to your heart. You ask if in composing this symphony I had a special programme in view. To such questions regarding my symphonic works I generally answer: nothing of the kind. In reality it is very difficult to answer this question . . .

Our symphony has a programme. That is to say, it is possible to express its contents in words, and I will tell you — and you alone — the meaning of the entire work and of its separate movements. Naturally I can only do so as regards its general features. The introduction is the germ, the leading idea of the whole work. This is Fate, that inevitable force which checks our aspirations towards happiness before they reach the goal, which watches jealously lest our peace and bliss should be complete and cloudless — a force which, like the sword of Damocles, hangs perpetually over our heads and is always embittering the soul. This force is inescapable and invincible. There is no other course but to submit and inwardly lament.

The sense of hopeless despair grows stronger and more poignant. Is it not better to turn from reality and lose ourselves in dreams? O! Joy, A sweet and tender dream enfolds me. A bright and serene presence leads me on. How wonderful! How remotely now is heard the first theme of the Allegro! Deeper and deeper the soul is sunk in dreams. All that was dark and joyless is forgotten. Here is happiness!

It is but a dream, Fate awakens us roughly.

So all life is but a continual alternation between grim truth and fleeting dreams of happiness. There is no haven. The waves drive us hither and thither, until the sea engulfs us. This is, approximately the programme of the first movement.

The second movement expresses another phase of suffering. Now it is the melancholy which steals over us when at evening we sit indoors alone, weary of work, while the book we have picked up for relaxation slips unheeded from our fingers. A long procession of old memories goes by. How sad to think how much is already *past and gone!* And yet these recollections of youth are sweet. We regret the past, although we have neither courage nor desire to start a new life. We are rather weary of existence. We would fain rest awhile and look back, recalling many things. There were moments when young blood pulsed warm through our veins and life gave all we asked. There were also moments of sorrow, irreparable loss. All this has receded so far into the past. How sad, yet sweet to lose ourselves therein!

In the third movement no definite feelings find expression. Here we have only capricious arabesques, intangible forms, which come into a man's head when he has been drinking wine and his nerves are rather excited. His mood is neither joyful nor sad. He thinks of nothing in particular. His fancy is free to follow its own flight, and it designs the strangest patterns. Suddenly memory calls up the picture of a tipsy peasant and a street song. From afar come the sounds of a military band. These are the kind of confused images which pass through our brains as we fall asleep. They have no connection with actuality, but are simply wild, strange, and bizarre.

The fourth movement. If you can find no reason for happiness in yourself, look at others. Go to the people. See how they can enjoy life and give themselves up entirely to festivity. A rustic holiday is depicted. Hardly

Page from a letter from Tchaikovsky to Madame von Meck 28 December 1877

have we had time to forget ourselves in the spectacle of other people's pleasure, when indefatigable Fate reminds us once more of its presence. Others pay no heed to us. They do not spare us a glance, nor stop to observe that we are lonely and sad. How merry, how glad they all are! All their feelings are so inconsequent, so simple. And will you still say that all the world is immersed in sorrow? Happiness does exist, simple and unspoilt. Be glad in others' gladness. This makes life possible.

I can tell you no more, dear friend, about the symphony. Naturally my description is not very clear or satisfactory. But there lies the peculiarity of instrumental music; we cannot analyse it. 'Where words leave off, music begins,' as Heine has said . . .

P.S. — Just as I was putting my letter into the envelope I began to read it again, and to feel misgivings as to the confused and incomplete programme which I am sending you. For the first time in my life I have attempted to put my musical thoughts and forms into words and phrases. I have not been very successful. I was horribly out of spirits all the time I was composing this symphony last winter, and this is a true echo of my feelings at the time. But only an echo. How is it possible to reproduce it in clear and definite language? I do not know. I have already forgotten a good deal. Only the general impression of my passionate and sorrowful experiences has remained. I am very, very anxious to know what my friends in Moscow say of my work.

The letter from which this long extract is given was dated 1 March, by which time Tchaikovsky had moved to Florence. Exactly a month earlier he had completed *Eugene Onegin* and had sent the score to Moscow. 'This opera has no future,' he later told Taneyev, 'I was quite aware of this when I wrote it. Nevertheless, I completed it and shall give it to the world if Jurgenson is willing to publish it.' With the symphony and the opera behind him, Tchaikovsky was content to rest in Florence and to enjoy life there. He settled down to read Schopenhauer's *'The World as Will and Idea'*, a copy of which Nadezhda Filaretovna had sent him, describing the book as a 'brilliant paradox'. Now, six months after the appalling crisis, he was able to describe his mood as 'rose-coloured', and he attributed his recovery to three people — Modest, Anatol and, of course, Nadezdha Filaretovna herself.

By mid-March Tchaikovsky had returned to Clarens with Modest, Kondrati and Alexey Sofronov. Kotek came to visit them and together they played through a great deal of new music, including Lalo's *Symphonie Espagñol*, about which Tchaikovsky became very enthusiastic. Most probably this inspired him to sketch out the Violin Concerto while he was still engrossed in the composition of the G minor Piano Sonata. He confessed to Nadezhda Filaretovna that 'for the first time in my life, I have begun to work on a new piece before finishing the one in hand'. By the beginning of April the sketches of the Concerto were complete, and Kotek, who it was intended should give the first performance, had mastered the first movement. The second movement displeased both violinist and composer, so Tchaikovsky replaced it with the present *Canzonetta*, and on 11 April the orchestration was finished. Kotek, however, was to lose interest in the work, and Tchaikovsky dedicated it to Leopold Auer who declared it impossible to play. It

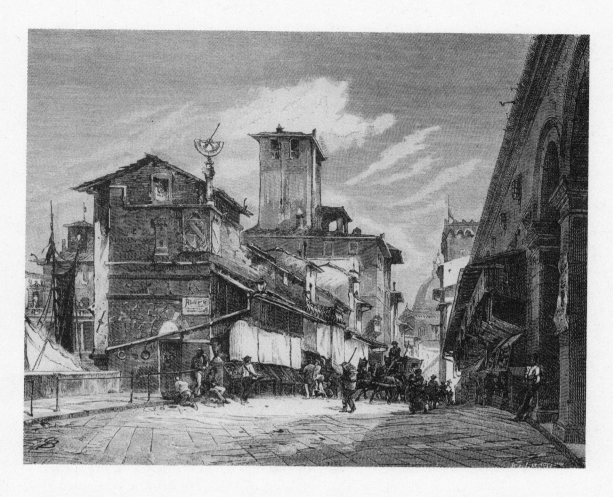

The Ponte Vecchio,
Florence 1876

was not until the end of 1881 that the Concerto received its première in Vienna performed by Adolf Brodsky.

Meanwhile Nikolay Rubinstein had played the First Piano Concerto on 22 March in Moscow. His change of attitude to the work delighted Tchaikovsky: 'I was convinced from the first that N.G. [Rubinstein] would play it splendidly. The work was originally intended for him, and took into consideration his immense virtuosity'. In similar fashion, Leopold Auer eventually became one of the most ardent champions of the Violin Concerto.

The time when Tchaikovsky had to think about his return to Russia was fast approaching, and the prospect filled him with misgivings. He was enjoying his new-found freedom, and letters to Nadezhda Filaretovna written from Clarens give the first hint of his wish to resign his post at the Conservatoire:

How unpleasant teaching will be after these months of freedom. I can give you no adequate idea how derogatory this kind of work can be to a man who has not the smallest vocation for it.

81

He was also depressed over news of serious political unrest in Russia. A campaign of socialist terrorism, begun earlier in the year, was gaining momentum, with an aim of inciting the peasants to revolt, and to paralyse the government by the assassination of high officials. Reluctantly Tchaikovsky began his homeward journey, lamenting the 'poisonous, malicious and abominable slanders' that filled the pages of Western newspapers. From Vienna on 20 April, he wrote Nadezhda Filaretovna that he was however returning 'a sound, sane man, full of renewed strength and energy'. Four days later he arrived at Kamenka.

Much relieved that the Davidovs greeted him with their usual degree of warmth, he immediately started work. By the end of the month the new Piano Sonata was complete, as well as 'The Twelve Pieces of Moderate Difficulty' Op 40, for piano. He had also begun a collection of twenty-four miniature piano pieces for children, called *Children's Album*, and planned to set the 'entire Liturgy of St. John Chrysostom'. The unresolved matter of his wife was left in the capable hands of Anatol, who had travelled to Moscow to press Antonina into suing for divorce. Nadezhda von Meck had offered 10,000 roubles for a quick settlement, and in an attempt to ease Tchaikovsky's growing nervousness over the matter she invited him to spend a few weeks at her country estate in Brailov. Needless to say, she had no intention of staying there herself. Gratefully he accepted and, amid the 'glorious' surroundings, completed the *Liturgy* and wrote three miniatures for violin and piano, published collectively as *Souvenir d'un Lieu* (one of these pieces was actually the discarded *Andante* from the Violin Concerto). His mind was never very far from opera, and he began searching once again for suitable subjects. He considered *Undine*, but afterwards was carried away by the idea of *Romeo and Juliet* — 'nothing but love, love, love'. He played through the whole of *Eugene Onegin* and admitted in a letter to Modest, that it 'had moved him to tears . . . if only the audiences of the future will feel towards the music as the composer does himself'.

On 13 June he made his first appearance in Moscow for almost a year. He had completely forgotten that the following day was Nikolay Rubinstein's birthday and, as was the custom in Russia, he would certainly be expected to attend the celebrations. His colleagues welcomed him warmly, but in Rubinstein's face he could detect a look of disapproval. 'He cannot forgive me for refusing to be a delegate to Paris,' he commented to Nadezhda Filaretovna, 'which from his point of view, I ought to have accepted as a great kindness. He doesn't like those who do not feel in his debt; he would prefer everyone around him to be known as his creations. In brief, I am *persona non grata* to him, and he couldn't hide it.' The birthday celebrations were a brief distraction

Nadezhda Filaretovna von Meck

Tchaikovsky in 1879

from the real reason for Tchaikovsky's presence in Moscow: the divorce. The Clerk of the Consistory informed him that a confrontation with Antonina was mandatory by law. But she was nowhere to be found, and Tchaikovsky seized the opportunity of escaping to Kamenka, leaving the matter in the hands of Jurgenson. When Antonina was eventually discovered, she flatly refused to sue for divorce on the only legal grounds possible at the time, adultery, obstinately claiming her husband to be innocent of such a charge. Jurgenson was too frightened to proceed any further for fear of scandal and persuaded her to leave Moscow in return for money. The way was clear for Tchaikovsky to return safely to Moscow, and by the middle of September, after brief visits to Brailov and Nizy where he had begun sketching the *First Suite* for Orchestra, he arrived in the city with the intention of informing Nikolay Rubinstein that he had made up his mind to resign from the Conservatoire.

Chapter 8

The Nomad

'I have written much that is beautiful — but how weak, how lacking in mastery' — Tchaikovsky

Having braced himself to tell Nikolay Rubinstein that he intended to resign from the Conservatoire, Tchaikovsky was disappointed to find on his arrival in Moscow that his Director had left the city. By an ironic twist, Rubinstein had gone to France to assume the rôle which Tchaikovsky had spurned, as official Russian delegate to the Paris Exhibition. The composer found himself in an embarrassing position. He could not proffer his resignation to anyone other than Rubinstein, especially in view of all the support, encouragement and friendship which over the years he had received from him. So he had little option but to settle down and take up his teaching duties once again at the commencement of term. This did not prevent him, however, from describing the Conservatoire (in a letter written to Modest) as a 'dirty, foetid, disgusting jail'.

Matters were made no easier when, on his return to Moscow, Rubinstein delivered a speech in which he heaped praise on the composer's work, and described in glowing terms the warmth with which his music had been received by audiences in Paris. So great was the encomium, that loud and prolonged applause broke out quite spontaneously as Rubinstein ended his speech. As Tchaikovsky explained to Nadezdha Filaretovna:

I need hardly tell you how painful this speech and the ovation were. But the following day, I informed him of my plans. I expected Nikolay Rubinstein to be indignant, and to do his utmost to persuade me that it would be better for me to stay on. But he merely remarked that the Conservatoire would lose a great deal of its prestige with the withdrawal of my name — which was as good as saying that the pupils would not really suffer much by my resignation. Probably he is right, for I am a poor and inexperienced teacher. But I anticipated greater opposition to my resignation.

Nursing his wounded pride, Tchaikovsky left Moscow and the Conservatoire on 19 October 1878 and made his way to St.

View of Florence from the
Terrace of San Miniato
about 1880

Petersburg, where he stayed for three weeks. Here he was offered a less onerous and more rewarding post at the local Conservatoire. But Tchaikovsky was in no mood to take up teaching in the capital having so recently escaped from his burdensome duties in Moscow, and the offer was rejected. From St. Petersburg he journeyed on to Kamenka where he stayed for a short time with the Davidovs before making his way back to Florence. And so began his long nomadic existence, during which he travelled constantly between Russia and the rest of Europe, never staying long in any one place and avoiding social contact as much as possible.

In Florence an apartment had already been rented for him by Madame von Meck who was herself on holiday there. On his arrival, Tchaikovsky found a note of welcome from her which gave precise timings of her daily walks to make quite certain that they would not meet. Despite these precautions they met face-to-face for the first time, quite by chance, although it is possible that Madame von Meck remained unaware of the encounter as she was extremely short-sighted. Other accidental meetings followed, but not once did they speak. Instead, they delighted in exchanging notes by messenger in which each commented on the other's actions and appearance. Tchaikovsky responded well to the atmosphere of Florence and began work on the orchestration of his *First Suite*. His morale was given a further boost when news reached him from St. Petersburg of a triumphant performance of the Fourth Symphony, and his thoughts turned yet again to opera. The inspiration of the new work was the martyrdom of St. Joan as described by Schiller in *Die Jungfrau von Orleans*. Tchaikovsky had come across this text in a Russian translation by Zhikovsky, and determined to use it as a basis for a libretto which he would write

85

himself. However, he quickly found that life in Florence offered too many distractions, and on 9 January 1879 he took up residence once again in the Villa Richelieu at Clarens in order to concentrate on the new project in peace and solitude. Eleven days later he was still in difficulty, as this extract from a letter to Madame von Meck reveals:

How often I jump up in sheer despair because I cannot find a rhyme, or the metre goes wrong, or because I have absolutely no notion what this or that character would say at a particular moment. I think it would be a blessing if someone were to publish a rhyming dictionary.

By mid-February, Tchaikovsky had moved on to Paris, where he 'lived the life of a hermit' until the opera was finished 'quite unexpectedly' on 5 March. He describes his feelings in a letter to Modest:

To squeeze music out of one's brain every day for ten weeks is indeed an exhausting business. Now I can breathe freely! Yesterday, I walked about Paris feeling quite another man.

He was also excited by the prospect of hearing Colonne conduct *The Tempest*, but his excitement turned to disappointment when the performance was greeted by 'feeble applause mingled with two or three audible hisses'. Hurriedly, Tchaikovsky packed his bags and made arrangements to return to Moscow. But before leaving Paris he wrote a letter of thanks to Colonne in which he declared that the failure was in no way due to his 'splendid' performance: it was the work itself which was 'diffuse in form and lacking in

Students of the Moscow Conservatoire presenting 'Eugene Onegin' in 1879

proportion'. Doubtless by somewhat unscrupulous means this letter fell into the hands of the *Gazette Musicale*, where it was published under the equivocal caption — 'a rare witness to the noble and sincere modesty of a composer'.

Back in Moscow, rehearsals had already begun for the première of *Eugene Onegin* at the Conservatoire. Tchaikovsky was impressed with the orchestra and chorus but thought the soloists 'left much to be desired'. Nikolay Rubinstein claimed to have 'fallen in love' with the opera and Taneyev, in an attempt to express his feelings after hearing the first act, could only 'burst into tears'. The première took place on 29 March, and even Anton Rubinstein travelled specially from St. Petersburg to attend. Before the performance Tchaikovsky was escorted back-stage where, to his horror, he found himself 'confronted by the whole Conservatoire' and presented with a wreath 'amid hearty applause'. The ovation was repeated at the end of the performance, but Tchaikovsky sensed that the applause was for him, and not for the work. Anton Rubinstein remained conspicuously silent, and only on his return to St. Petersburg did he comment to his wife that *Onegin* was completely lacking in 'grand opera style'. The production had undoubtedly suffered at the hands of amateurs and the critics were generally agreed that the work was of little artistic value. Only one press review predicted the opera's future success: 'In spite of its lack of dramatic life, Tchaikovsky's work will probably become one of the most popular pieces of our operatic repertoire, thanks to its national subject and excelling music', wrote the critic of *Russkiye Vyedomosti*.

The failure of *Onegin* soon faded into the background, for when Tchaikovsky returned to St. Petersburg he was faced with a far more urgent problem: Antonina. During his absence, she had been seen watching the house in which he shared a flat with Anatol. One afternoon Tchaikovsky found his wife waiting for him on his return, and she subjected him to a torrent of hysterical abuse which went on for two hours or more. Only when she was offered a sum of money to return to Moscow did she calm down. But she remained quite adamant in her refusal to sue Tchaikovsky for divorce, claiming that he was still passionately in love with her. It is not difficult to imagine Tchaikovsky's frantic efforts to bring this painful interview to an end, or his horror when he later discovered that his wife, instead of returning to Moscow as she had promised, used the money to rent a flat in the same building. As soon as she moved in the hysterical onslaught was resumed, and the unfortunate composer was showered with abusive letters and threatening demands for money. In desperation, he fled to Moscow. Antonina promptly followed him to keep up the attack. At this point Tchaikovsky — not for the first time in his life — sought refuge with the Davidovs at Kamenka, beyond the reach of his over-wrought wife. Here at least he was safe, and shortly after his arrival on 21 April he settled down once more to the task of orchestrating the *First Suite* and the new opera, which he entitled *The Maid of Orleans*.

By way of welcome contrast, good news started to arrive from western Europe. His *Rococo Variations* were received with great enthusiasm at the Wiesbaden Festival by an audience which included the venerable Franz Liszt who declared, 'at last, here is music again'. At the same Festival Hans von Bülow gave a perform-ance of the first Piano Concerto to great acclaim, following his recent success in London with the première of the same work. Colonne wrote from Paris that, despite the failure of *The Tempest*, a substantial number of works by Tchaikovsky were scheduled for future concerts. Nearer home, at Kiev, a performance of the *Liturgy* had at last taken place in the University chapel. The long delay had been caused by the high-handed action of the director of the Imperial Chapel who had confiscated the score. The faithful Jurgenson, acting on Tchaikovsky's behalf as his publisher, promptly sued the authorities for its return, and his action had been successfully upheld by the courts. As he explained to Madame von Meck — 'only those works which have been recognised by the chapel can be publicly sold or performed. That is the reason why, until now, no Russian composers have written music for the church.'

By August 1879 Act 3 of *The Maid of Orleans* was finished, and Tchaikovsky accepted an invitation from Madame von Meck to stay at Brailov once again. On this occasion, however, he was offered rooms not in the main house, as she was herself in residence there, but in a small cottage on the estate at a village called Simaki. Immediately he fell under the spell of 'the very, very old house' with its secluded garden surrounded by 'ancient oaks and lime trees'. On the other hand he was troubled by the 'close proximity' of his benefactress whom, as he wrote to Modest, he preferred to regard as a 'kind of remote and invisible angel'. As before, the most elaborate precautions were taken during his three-week stay to avoid the possibility of a chance meeting, although there were now strong hints that Madame von Meck wished their friendship to assume a somewhat different character. For example, she suggested that her youngest daughter, Milochka, should visit Tchaikovsky, but he was quick to reply that such a move would threaten their relationship which, by its very nature, was so precious to him. Next, came an invitation to visit the main house while she was away: to this Tchaikovsky readily agreed, and at the appointed time he spent two hours wandering about the rooms in the carefully-planned absence of the mistress of Brailov. Then one afternoon,

Franz Liszt (1811-1886), Hungarian pianist and composer

The Tchaikovsky brothers: Anatol, Nikolay, Hippolyte, Peter, Modest

The opera house in St. Petersburg

despite his strict adherence to the timed programme, Tchaikovsky met Madame von Meck during a walk in the woods. He described the encounter in a letter to Anatol:

It was an awkward predicament. Although we were face to face for only a moment, I felt horribly confused. However, I raised my hat politely. She seemed to lose her head completely and did not know what to do.

Tchaikovsky hurried back to the cottage, and immediately wrote a letter of apology. Back came a disconcerting reply:

I felt so gay and happy that tears came to my eyes . . . I do not seek any close personal relationship with you, but I love to be near you passively, tacitly . . . To feel you, not as a myth, but as a living man whom I love sincerely.

We do not know what passed in Tchaikovsky's mind as he made his return journey to St. Petersburg with the completed scores of the *First Suite* and *The Maid of Orleans*, but on 26 September he received a further letter from Madame von Meck which could have done little to reassure him:

I doubt that you can ever understand how intensely jealous I am of you despite the absence of personal contact between us. Do you know, I am jealous in the least forgivable way, as a woman is jealous of the man she loves? Do you know, when you married, it was intensely difficult for me, as though some part of my heart had broken? The thought that you were near that woman was bitter and unbearable. And do you realize how wicked I am? I was glad when you were unhappy with her! I blamed myself for that feeling. I don't believe that I gave myself away at all, and yet I could not quell my feelings. They are not to be commanded. I hated that woman because she did not make you happy, but I should have hated her a hundred times more if you had found happiness with her. I believed that she had robbed me of what should be mine alone, what is rightfully mine for the reason that I love you more than anyone and value you above anything else in the world. If knowing this upsets you, forgive my unintentional confessions. I have said them. The symphony was the cause. Still, I think that it is better for you to realize that I am no such idealist as you picture. And then, it can't alter any part of our relationship. I want no change. I should like to be assured that nothing will be altered as I come to the end of my life . . . But that I have no right to say.

Tchaikovsky's suspicions were confirmed: Nadezdha Filaretovna had at last over-played her hand by allowing their strange relationship, which had now reached its emotional climax, to become too intimate or, at the very least, her confessions to become too outspoken. The composer sensed danger and characteristically backed away, insisting that the love he felt for her could be 'expressed in no way other than music'.

Subdued by his reply, Madame von Meck responded by offering to arrange and finance a performance of the Fourth Symphony in Paris, and although he doubted that the work would achieve any success there Tchaikovsky accepted her generosity. By the time he received news of Colonne's agreement to conduct the Symphony at one of his concerts, Tchaikovsky was once more in Kamenka. Content at first to idle away the time, he soon became bored. 'I realised that I wanted work', he wrote to his patroness on 24 October, 'and began to occupy myself. The boredom relieved'. He had started work on a second Piano Concerto, in G minor, which he completed during a three-week stay in Paris that November. At that time, alarming news of an unsuccessful attempt on the life of the Tsar spread across Europe and prompted Tchaikovsky to write Nadezhda Filaretovna one of his rare political comments: 'so long as all of us — the citizens of Russia — are not called to take part in the government of the country, there is no hope for a better future'.

From Paris Tchaikovsky journeyed on to Rome in the company of Modest, Kondrati and Alexey Sofronov. Here, more disturbing news from Russia awaited him — this time of a more personal nature. Nikolay Rubinstein had written to complain that the *First Suite*, the première of which he had given in Moscow during the month of December, was 'awkward'. While he was always prepared to criticise his own works, Tchaikovsky did not take kindly to criticism from others. To let off steam he wrote a somewhat petulant letter to Jurgenson in which he said, among other things —

... either Rubinstein is mistaken, or I must give up composing altogether — one or the other. The one interest which binds me to life is centred on my compositions: every first performance marks an epoch for me. Can no one understand that it would have been a joy to have received a few words of appreciation? I feel as sick as a dog. Either I have never understood anything about the orchestra, or the criticism of my Suite is on a par with N.R's remarks about my pianoforte concerto in 1875 — that it was impracticable. But what was impossible in 1875 turned out to be quite possible in 1878.

In point of fact the *First Suite* was very well received at its Moscow première, but Rubinstein's criticisms, and those of Taneyev ('the difficulties are chiefly centred in the woodwind'), had revived bitter memories.

Within a short space of time, Jurgenson received a second letter from Rome (dated 23 January 1880) in which Tchaikovsky complained about his health. He was clearly upset by the news which he had received on the previous day of his father's death — 'it is a bitter grief that I shall never see him again'. To add to his sorrow, he also had word from Kamenka that his sister Alexandra was far from well. However, he worked steadily at the second Piano

Tchaikovsky in 1880

Concerto, and completely revised the second Symphony, for which he wrote an entirely new first movement ('greatly inferior to the original', noted Taneyev sternly). Italian folk songs which could be heard everywhere in Rome inspired him to sketch out the popular *Italian Capriccio*, which opens with the trumpet-call he heard each morning from a cavalry barracks near his apartment.

Elsewhere in Europe, there were many encouraging signs that his reputation was growing. Although Colonne's performance of the Fourth Symphony in Paris had been greeted with 'icy coldness', both the Third String Quartet and the *Sérénade Mélancolique* had scored a major success in the city. The first Piano Concerto had been triumphantly acclaimed in Berlin, Budapest and New York, whence Walter Damrosch had also sent congratulations to Tchaikovsky on his *First Suite*. In March 1880, the composer returned to St. Petersburg to await the Opera directorate's verdict on *The Maid of Orleans*. Immediately on his arrival, much to his displeasure, he was swamped by a large number of social and official engagements. To avoid these many commitments he fled to Moscow, but found little respite there:

I have hardly been out of a tail coat and white tie, associating with the most august personages. It is all very flattering, sometimes touching, but exhausting to the last degree.

He escaped to Kamenka with a feeling of great relief, but on his arrival on 23 April he found commitments of a different kind waiting for him. Alexandra and her husband took the opportunity of going away together for a brief holiday, leaving their young and lively family to the composer's charge. Fortunately, 'uncle Peter' was extremely fond of his nephews and nieces and probably enjoyed their boisterous company a great deal more than the demanding social life of Moscow and St. Petersburg. At all events, he was able to complete the orchestration of the *Italian Capriccio* and to make substantial revisions to the opera which, to his satisfaction, had now been accepted by the authorities in St. Petersburg.

Midsummer of that year saw him once again at Brailov as a guest of Madame von Meck. Here he had a long-awaited opportunity of going carefully through her vast music-library — an exercise which filled him with gloom and dissatisfaction about his own output, as we learn from a letter to Modest:

I have written much that is beautiful — but how weak, how lacking in mastery . . . I have made up my mind to write nothing new for a time, and to devote myself to re-editing and to correcting my earlier works.

From Brailov he moved to the isolated cottage at Simaki where he finished correcting *The Maid of Orleans* and resumed his study of

91

Anton Rubinstein (after a
photograph by Ganz,
Brussels)

the English language. It was one of his great ambitions to be able to
read the works of Shakespeare, Dickens and Thackeray in their original tongue.

The resolution which he made at Brailov did not last long, for
on his return to Kamenka at the beginning of August he started
work on two new projects. The first was the *1812 Overture*, written
at Rubinstein's insistence to commemorate the Tsar's silver
jubilee: Tchaikovsky himself regarded it as '. . . very noisy. I wrote
it without much warmth or enthusiasm, and it therefore has no
great artistic value'. By way of complete contrast however, the
second of the new projects became one of the composer's favourite
works, written — as he put it from 'an inward pulse'. This was the
Serenade for Strings, Op 48, which drew wholehearted approval
even from the composer's severest critic, Anton Rubinstein. His
brother Nikolay gave the first performance of the *Italian Capriccio*
in Moscow on 15 December to a delighted audience but to a less
enthusiastic press, whose reviewers criticised the work for its
'coarse and cheap' effects. A few weeks later the piece was given at

Opening measures from the *1812 Overture*

Scene from *The Maid of Orleans* in first performance at the Marinski Theatre in St. Petersburg, 1881

Brailov estate of N. von Meck

St. Petersburg with much the same result. Cui, for example, considered it 'no work of art, but a valuable gift to those who build programmes for open-air concerts'.

Meanwhile, rehearsals were under way at the Bolshoi for the first professional production of *Eugene Onegin*. The opening night on 23 January 1881 was not the triumphant success which had been so confidently expected, but the work nevertheless gradually found its own audience. Tchaikovsky himself was much more concerned about his later opera *The Maid of Orleans*, rehearsals for which were not going well at St. Petersburg. There was constant bickering among the singers with whom Tchaikovsky was far from satisfied, and the authorities made cuts in the production budget to compensate for serious over-expenditure on a recently-presented ballet. To make matters worse Napravnik, to whom the opera was dedicated, insisted on making his customary cuts and revisions to the score itself. At its première on 25 February, Tchaikovsky took no fewer than twenty-four curtain calls, and he departed for Italy the following day quite convinced that his latest work was a triumph. He had not reckoned with the critics however, for with Cui at their head they kept up a torrent of critical abuse which eventually forced the Opera directors to withdraw the production, in spite of full houses.

When he reached Rome, Tchaikovsky was lionised by the many members of the Russian nobility who lived in the city. All this he found quite objectionable: 'O Society! What can be more appalling, duller, more intolerable? May the Devil take them all!' Jurgenson wrote from Moscow saying that Tchaikovsky now had grounds for divorce, since Antonina had taken a lover and had a child by him. But the composer was reluctant to have the affair dragged through the courts for fear of what his wife might reveal. So wisely he decided to leave matters well alone. Then on 13 March came news which most of Europe had been expecting for some time: Tsar Alexander II had been assassinated. 'At such moments as these,' Tchaikovsky wrote to Madame von Meck, 'it is very miserable to be abroad. I long to be in Russia.' Ten days later Nikolay Rubinstein died suddenly in Paris and Tchaikovsky at once hurried to the French capital where 'much to his shame', as he later confessed to Modest, he 'suffered less from the sense of irreparable loss, than from the horror of seeing poor Rubinstein's body'. He stayed long enough to attend the funeral of his friend, and to see the wooden coffin placed on a train on the first stage of its journey back to Russia.

A few weeks later Tchaikovsky himself, still in a depressed state of mind, made his way back to Moscow, where he was alarmed to hear rumours concerning the imminent bankruptcy of Madame von Meck. He wrote to her at once, and she confirmed that her son,

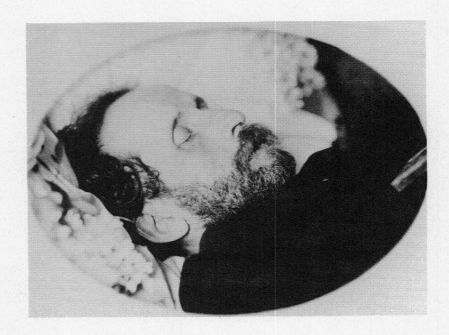

Nikolay Rubinstein in his
coffin

Vladimir, had lost her millions of roubles, but she insisted that
Tchaikovsky's annuity was not in jeopardy. Despite her assurances,
he gloomily told Modest that he would soon be forced to take up
teaching again: at the same time, he rejected 'most emphatically' an
offer to succeed Nikolay Rubinstein as Director of the Moscow
Conservatoire.

Most of the summer of 1881 was spent at Kamenka, but without
'the slightest inclination' to compose. He kept himself busy by
studying Russian church music, and by editing the works of
Dimitry Bortniansky (1752-1825) — a task which he found highly
irksome, but which he had undertaken for Jurgenson in order to
earn some money. So anxious was he about his financial position
that he wrote secretly to the Tsar who awarded him a grant of 3000
roubles. The only new project he had in mind at this time was to
compose yet another opera: he still hankered after a great operatic
success. By the time he left for Rome at the end of November, he
had more or less made up his mind to base the new work on
Pushkin's *Poltava*.

Soon after his return to Italy he learned about Brodsky's première
of the Violin Concerto in Vienna, which had caused a sensational
uproar. Among the reviews was this scathing attack by Hanslick:

The violin is no longer played, but torn apart, beaten black and blue . . .
Friedrich Fischer, describing obscene paintings, once said that there were
pictures 'one could see stink'. For the first time, Tchaikovsky's violin
concerto brings us face to face with this question: may there not also be
musical compositions which we can hear stink?

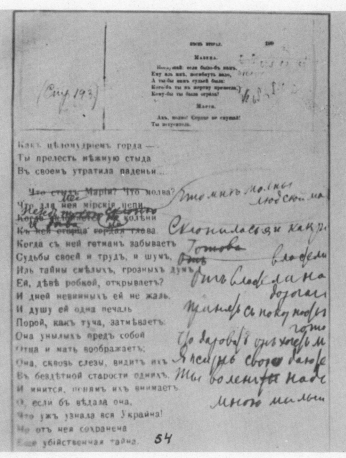

Poltava by Pushkin, with sketch of libretto and music themes by Tchaikovsky

B.B. Korcov in the title role for first performance of *Mazeppa* at the Bolshoi Theatre in Moscow, 1884

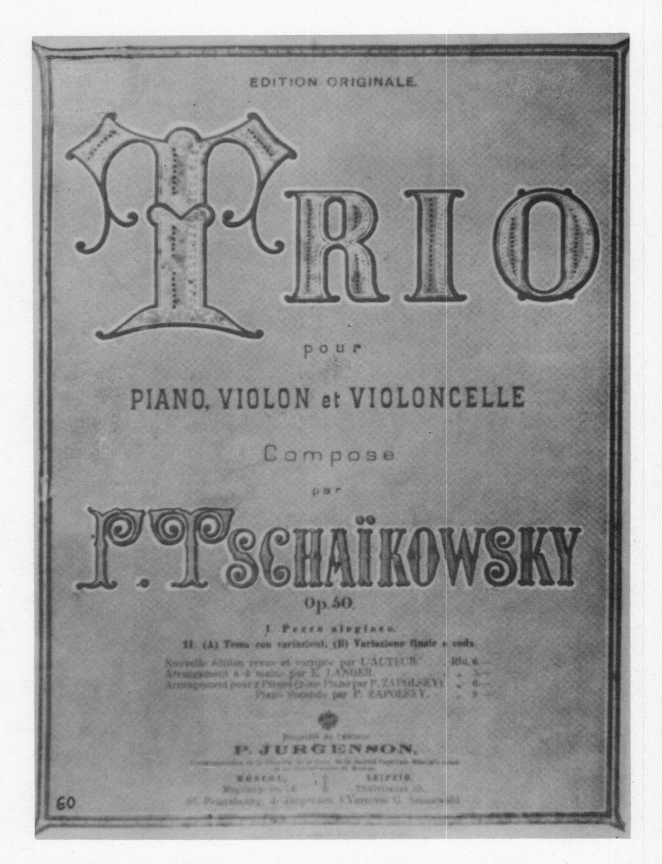

Title page for the original edition of the trio written by Tchaikovsky "in memory of the great artist" as influenced by the death of N.G. Rubinstein

According to Modest, Tchaikovsky never forgot these words and 'knew them by heart'. Angry and depressed, he wrote to Jurgenson expressing indignation at the withdrawal of both *Eugene Onegin* and *The Maid of Orleans* from the current repertoire, and lamenting the fact that neither the Second Piano Concerto nor the Violin Concerto had yet been performed in Russia. But clearly what upset him most was the news that the directors of the Opera had set aside a sum of 30,000 roubles for a production of Rimsky-Korsakov's opera *The Snow Maiden*, a subject he regarded as very much his own:

Is it not equally unpleasant to you to feel that 'our' subject has been taken away from us, and that we shall now sing new music to old words? . . . I could cry with mortification.

Tchaikovsky sought consolation in his work and early in 1882 started to compose a piano trio, more as an experiment than as a serious work of composition. Many years earlier, when Madame von Meck tried to commission a chamber piece on similar lines, he told her that he disliked that particular combination of instruments. Nevertheless, within weeks of embarking upon the project, Tchaikovsky had completed a Trio in A minor. It turned out to be a work of considerable length, and he was not at all confident of its success. 'I may have arranged music of a symphonic character as a trio', he wrote to Madame von Meck, 'instead of writing directly for my instruments. I have tried to avoid this.' He dedicated the trio (Op 50) to 'the memory of a great artist' and it is, indeed, both a masterpiece among his chamber works and a remarkable tribute to the memory of Nikolay Rubinstein.

After the piano trio was completed inspiration ran dry, and Tchaikovsky took himself off to Naples, accompanied by Modest and Kondrati, in a restless and discontented frame of mind. By the middle of April he was back in Russia to attend family celebrations for the marriage of his brother, Anatol. Early in May he retreated once more to Kamenka, where he took up his new opera, now to be called *Mazeppa*, with a singular lack of enthusiasm. During the summer months of 1882 an Art and Industrial Exhibition was held in Moscow during the course of which important first performances of his works were given. At the opening concert on 30 May Taneyev performed the Piano Concerto No. 2, which was well received by an enthusiastic audience. Suitably encouraged, Tchaikovsky allowed himself to be persuaded to attend in person a concert devoted entirely to his own works, at which the *1812 Overture* and the Violin Concerto were heard in Moscow for the first time. These, too, met with considerable success although some dissenting voices were heard: one critic went so far as to suggest that

95

Tchaikovsky's favourite
pupil, Serge Taneyev
(1856-1915)

the composer was now 'played out'. Another première during the summer season was that of the *Serenade for Strings*, which won immediate and wide acclaim from audiences and musicians alike. It should have been a rewarding and exciting time for the composer but, as he confessed to Modest, he found Moscow heavy and oppressive:

It all lies in the fact that life is impossible for me, except in the country or abroad. Why this is, God knows — but I am simply on the verge of insanity. This undefinable, horrible, torturing malady, which declares itself in the fact that I cannot live a day or even an hour in either of the Russian capitals without suffering, will perhaps be explained to me in some better world.

As soon as it was possible to do so, Tchaikovsky hurried back to Kamenka to resume work on *Mazeppa*. Progress was, however, painfully slow, and in September we find him complaining to Madame von Meck that never before had he found an opera so difficult to write, and expressing fears that the lack of progress was probably due to his 'diminishing creative powers'. On 30 October, the Trio in A minor, Op 50, was performed for the first time in Moscow: once again, the work was successful with the audience, but not with the press. Taneyev wrote to Tchaikovsky assuring him that he had 'never experienced greater pleasure in studying a new composition.' Flattered by this remark, Tchaikovsky wrote a letter of thanks to Taneyev in which, among other things, he told him that *Mazeppa* was progressing 'tortoise-fashion'.

In January 1883 he made his annual pilgrimage to Paris, where he received two urgent commissions from Russia. The first was for a cantata, to be entitled *Moscow*, to celebrate the forthcoming coronation of Tsar Alexander III in May, and the second was for a new march to be performed a week after the coronation itself. He had already undertaken to arrange *Slavsya* from Glinka's *A Life for the Tsar* for a choral performance to be given by many thousands of voices, by way of spectacular greeting to the new Tsar and Tsarina. All three commissions he completed in Paris, as well as the score of *Mazeppa* itself. On his return to St. Petersburg late in May, Tchaikovsky carefully avoided the coronation celebrations, but took the opportunity of submitting the score of *Mazeppa* to the directors of the Opera before making his way to Kamenka. Here he worked on the Second Suite, Op 53, which was completed in October, and resumed his English studies.

Mazeppa was well received by the authorities who decided to stage a Moscow première on 15 February 1884, to be followed four days later by a first performance in St. Petersburg itself. The opening night in Moscow was a triumph, and Tchaikovsky was

The Tsar Alexander III

given a standing ovation at the end of the performance. However he was again convinced that the applause was for him personally and not for the work. Unable to face the première in St. Petersburg he fled to Paris. This was a serious mistake because the Tsar himself was present at this performance, and expressed 'extreme surprise' at the absence of the composer. Tchaikovsky was not reassured to receive letters from Modest, saying that the performance 'obtained a mere *succès d'estime*' and that it was generally condemned by the press, or from Jurgenson, who plainly told him that the opera had failed largely on account of his non-appearance. Napravnik advised Tchaikovsky to return home immediately as there was strong rumours that he was about to be presented to their Imperial Majesties. These rumours were well-founded, for a few days later it was announced that the Order of St. Vladimir (Fourth Class) was to be conferred on the composer. Unhappily, he was by then suffering from a severe chill, but well-dosed with bromide he arrived at Gatchina on 19 March to receive his award. 'I was first presented to the Emperor,' he later described to Anatol, 'and then to the Empress. Both were most friendly and kind. I think it is only necessary to look once into the Emperor's eyes to remain his most loyal admirer.' His absence from the St. Petersburg première of *Mazeppa* was delicately overlooked, and Tchaikovsky considered himself deeply honoured by such imperial approval. With his award he withdrew to Kamenka once again, in order to rest and to consider his next work.

The Maryinsky Theatre, St. Petersburg

Chapter 9

The Wanderer Returns

'How short life is! How much I still have to do, to think and to say! We keep putting things off and meanwhile death lurks round the corner.' — Tchaikovsky

From this point on, the diaries which Tchaikovsky carefully maintained become an increasingly important source of information, particularly as his lengthy correspondence with Madame von Meck declines. We learn, for example, that when he returned to Kamenka after receiving the Tsar's award he found it difficult to concentrate on new composition. An entry on 25 April 1884 mentions work on another piano concerto which he describes as 'poor, and not original'. It was subsequently re-worked to become the *Concert Fantasia* Op 56, for piano and orchestra. Three days later we find:

In the forest and indoors I have been trying to lay the foundations of a new symphony, but I am not at all satisfied . . . Walked in the garden and found the germ, not of a symphony, but of a future Suite.

This *Third Suite* for orchestra did not make very satisfactory progress, and we can see the composer becoming increasingly perturbed about his failures:

Very dissatisfied because everything that comes into my head is so commonplace. Am I played out?

By 6 May, on the eve of his forty-fourth birthday, he had still not regained his self-confidence:

How much have I been through and — without false modesty — how little have I accomplished! In my actual vocation I must say, hand on heart, I have achieved nothing, perfected nothing which can serve as a model . . . The period of quiet, undisturbed existence is over for me. There remain agitation and conflict and much that I — such as I am — find it hard to endure. No: the time has come to live by *oneself*, and *in one's own way*!

Tchaikovsky in 1886

Scene from *Eugene Onegin* as performed at the "Estonia" Theatre in Tallin

View of Paris showing the Place du Carrousel

This is the first indication we have that Tchaikovsky was at last thinking of settling down in a home of his own. He elaborated the idea a few days later in a letter to Madame von Meck:

I wish only for a little house with a pretty garden, *not too new*. A *stream* is most desirable, as is a forest and a nearby railway station for easy access to Moscow.

But Madame von Meck had accommodation problems of her own. She had been forced to sell Brailov to cover her financial losses and had acquired a less sumptuous country estate at Pleschcheevo, to which Tchaikovsky was cordially invited. He accepted gratefully, and stayed until the end of October when a further production of *Eugene Onegin* was due to be given in St. Petersburg. He arrived in the capital only to find the old, familiar pattern was to repeat itself: the audience was ecstatic, but the critics distinctly cool. The formidable Cui referred to the opera's 'wearisome monotony', but on this occasion the critics failed to carry the day. From the second night onwards it became quite clear that *Eugene Onegin* was destined to become a considerable box-office success, and to take its place as the most popular Russian opera since Glinka's *A Life for the Tsar*. In many respects, this production of *Eugene Onegin* marked a turning point in Tchaikovsky's life, although it is likely that he did not fully realise it at the time. Modest had his feet rather more firmly on the ground when he pointed out that the success of the opera not only substantially increased Tchaikovsky's earnings, but also meant that:

. . . his name, hitherto known and respected among musicians and a fairly wide circle of musical amateurs, was now recognised by the great public and he acquired a popularity which no Russian composer before him had attained in his own country.

Tchaikovsky had other things on his mind: Kotek was dying of consumption at Davos in Switzerland, and after the second performance of the opera at St. Petersburg he hurried to his friend's bedside to pay his final respects. From Davos he wandered on to Paris with no clear purpose in mind, increasingly unhappy about his 'nomadic existence' and more determined than ever 'to have a *home*, be it in Kamenka or in Moscow'.

From Paris back to Moscow, where he told Alexey Sofronov to find a furnished house for him at a convenient, mid-way point between that city and St. Petersburg. The place chosen was Maidanovo, a village just outside Klin, and the house 'although not ideal, has beautifully furnished rooms and a fine view'. He rented it for a year, and formally took up residence in February 1885.

Shortly after moving in, he wrote to Modest:

I eat, walk and sleep when, and as much as, I please. In fact — I live.

He had good reason to be pleased. Quite apart from the triumph of *Eugene Onegin* and his growing fame throughout Russia, his Third Orchestral Suite had been rapturously received at its première under Hans von Bülow in St. Petersburg, and he had been elected unanimously Director of the Russian Musical Society in Moscow. At Maidanovo he started work on a long-cherished project — the complete revision of his favourite opera *Vakula the Smith*. By April, he had composed a number of completely new scenes:

All that was bad I threw out. What is good I have left . . . in a word I have done whatever is necessary to save the opera from the oblivion it has not deserved.

So substantial were the re-workings that he decided to re-name the opera *Cherevichki* (The Red Shoes) and as soon as the revised score was ready he took it to St. Petersburg in order to discuss its possible staging with the directors of the Opera. As he reported

Contemporary view of Paris

later to Madame von Meck, everything was settled 'beautifully' and he was promised a splendid new production. During his stay in the capital he celebrated his forty-fifth birthday with Anatol and, later, at a dinner given in his honour at the Conservatoire. In April he returned to Moscow to attend the annual examinations in his new capacity as Director of the Russian Musical Society. While he was there he was able to secure Taneyev's appointment as Director of the Conservatoire, in succession to Nikolay Rubinstein, and well satisfied with his efforts he returned to Maidanovo to start work on a new and important orchestral piece, *Manfred*.

The original idea for a symphonic work based on Byron's poem had been suggested to him three years earlier by Balakirev who, rather tactlessly, provided Tchaikovsky not only with a detailed programme for each of the four movements, but a complete key scheme as well. Not unnaturally, the composer lost interest, but when the matter was raised again by Balakirev in the winter of 1884, he promised that the work would be completed by not later than the following summer. It was a promise which he was to regret, as we can see from a letter written to Taneyev on 25 June:

I have made up my mind to compose *Manfred* because I shall find no rest until I have redeemed my promise, so rashly given to Balakirev last winter. I do not know how it will turn out, but in the meantime I am very discontented. No! It is a thousand times more pleasant to compose without a programme.

Despite his misgivings, Tchaikovsky managed to have the new score ready by September, He had followed Balakirev's programme very closely but feared that the end result was full of 'unusual intricacy and difficulty' and, for that reason, he was convinced that the new work would be played 'once or twice, and then disappear'. He was so convinced about its lack of popular appeal that he refused Jurgenson the publication rights, on the grounds that it would be quite impossible for his publisher to make any profit on the piece. And yet, perversely enough, he regarded *Manfred* as one of his better works.

During the course of its composition he had moved to an unfurnished house on the Maidanovo estate. In a letter to Madame von Meck, he described it as standing

somewhat apart from the rest, and a large piece of the garden is to be fenced in and kept for my special use. Although the neighbourhood is not what I could wish yet, taking into account the proximity of a large town with a railway station, I have decided to take the place for two years. It is pleasant and comfortable, and I think I shall feel happy here.

The decoration and the furnishing of the new house were left in the hands of his manservant Alexey Sofronov who, according to Modest, 'lacked any idea of beauty or of tastefulness'. As a result, he filled the place with very basic furniture and odd bits of rubbish. Tchaikovsky added to the chaos by 'purchasing the most unnecessary things' including 'two horses, which he had great difficulty subsequently in selling, and an old English clock that did not work'. Nevertheless he took great pride in his new possessions, proudly referring to them as 'my table-cloth', 'my dog' and 'my silver'. As Modest points out he was, apparently, 'as pleased as a child'. Only the most privileged guests, such as Kashkin, Taneyev, Hubert, Albrecht and Laroche were welcomed to the new house, and the composer found himself keeping to a strict daily routine which he observed, when at home, for the rest of his life.

It became his habit to rise between seven and eight o'clock in the morning, after which he would spend the next hour or so drinking tea, reading the Bible and other suitable works, or studying English. Before starting work at nine-thirty, he would take a short walk. Lunch followed at one o'clock, after which he would take a solitary walk lasting two hours, during which most of his creative work was done, jotting down ideas in a notebook, like Beethoven, or planning the construction of a new work. All these ideas would

Street scene in Tiflis c.1880

102

Steamship approaching the
Port of Batum c.1880

be sketched out at the piano the following morning. Then at four
o'clock he returned for tea and engaged in conversation with any
guests who happened to be present. At five o'clock he withdrew to
work for another two hours, after which he would take a further
walk, this time in company, before supper. At the end of the day he
would relax by reading, playing cards, talking or playing the piano
until eleven o'clock, at which time he would retire to his own room
either to write up his diary or to read before going to sleep. It was
from this period of his career onwards that Tchaikovsky refused to
allow anyone — not even his closest friends — to hear a new work
before publication.

With *Manfred* behind him, Tchaikovsky started work on another
opera *The Sorceress*. On 21 September he wrote to Madame von
Meck that 'the first act (the only one in hand) is splendid: life and
action in plenty. If nothing prevents me, I hope to have the
sketches ready by the Spring.' Within a fortnight the first act was
ready, and in a subsequent letter he said that 'he was growing more
and more enthusiastic over the task'. After this auspicious start he
encountered difficulties, and a further eighteen months were to
elapse before the opera was complete.

He stayed at Maidanovo until March 1886, when he left for
Moscow to attend the première of *Manfred*. It was given a first-rate
performance, and Tchaikovsky was confirmed in his belief that it
was his finest orchestral work to date. By a curious paradox, the
audience on this occasion was not enthusiastic, but the critics
acclaimed the new piece. Even Cui was moved to comment, later in
the year, that 'we must be grateful to Tchaikovsky for having en-
riched the treasury of our national symphonic music'. In spite of

103

his approval, and that of other critics, the work failed to find its place in the normal repertoire and fell into an obscurity from which it has only recently been rescued.

Any disappointment which Tchaikovsky may have felt was dispelled during a visit early the following month, with his brother Anatol, to Tiflis where he was treated as a major celebrity. The locals organised a concert of his works; and he was given a standing ovation as he entered his box at the concert house. Later, he was presented with a silver wreath, among other tributes, and at a meeting of the Tiflis Music Society a most laudatory speech was made in his honour. In a characteristic way, Tchaikovsky valued this spontaneous tribute from a remote provincial town far more than the plaudits he had hitherto received in Moscow and St. Petersburg. He was greatly flattered:

I count this month the happiest in my life. I have never experienced anything like it before . . . a glorious remembrance.

From Tiflis he journeyed to Batum, where he took the steamer *Armenia* to Marseilles, and then by train to Paris. During the

Marseilles

104

Edouard Lalo (1823-92)

Léo Delibes (1836-91)

voyage, he was struck by awe to see Mount Etna erupting. On his arrival at the French capital towards the end of May he spent a great deal of time at the opera and at the theatre and devoted himself to developing the third act of *The Sorceress*. He met both Lalo and Gabriel Fauré, and was 'deeply touched' when Delibes called on him. He also took the opportunity of talking to Colonne and to the distinguished violinist and conductor Lamoureux about future performances of his works in Paris. By June he was back at Maidanovo, writing to Madame von Meck on the pleasures of returning home:

How dear and cosy is my little house which, when I left, lay deep in snow and is now surrounded by foliage and flowers. The three months I spent abroad were lost time as regards work, but I feel I have gained in strength and can now devote my whole time to it without exhausting myself.

Work continued on *The Sorceress*, and he filled his diary with lengthy entries which touched on many subjects: the entry for 2 October reads: 'probably after my death it will be of interest to the world to hear of my musical predilections and prejudices'. Then follow some revealing notes about the major composers: Beethoven he praised 'unconditionally', although he 'could not love him'. Mozart he found 'the culminating point of all beauty in the sphere of music'. Their precursor, Bach, he enjoyed only because 'it is interesting to play a good fugue' and not because he considered him a great genius. As a composer he regarded Handel 'only fourth-rate: he is not even interesting'. Gluck, on the other hand, he found sympathetic, despite 'his poor creative gift'. 'Some works' of Haydn he thought were enjoyable. Brahms he considered to be a 'self-conscious mediocrity' and he was irritated that he 'should be recognised as a genius . . . so chaotic, so dry and so meaningless.'

After a severe attack of migraine in December, Tchaikovsky left for Moscow in order to conduct the première of *Cherevichki*. It was his first public performance on the podium for many years, and after the first rehearsal, which went extremely well, he was impressed by his own prowess. 'Now I know I *can* conduct,' he wrote triumphantly to Modest. The opening night was arranged for 31 January 1887, but that morning he woke up feeling 'really ill', and spent the day suffering 'indescribable mental agonies' which left him 'half-dead' by the time he reached the theatre in the evening. A cordial reception from the audience reassured him, and he went on to give a highly successful performance of the opera itself. Sad news awaited him on his return to Maidanovo: Alexandra's eldest daughter Tatiana had died at Kamenka. Nevertheless he plunged into the task of orchestrating *The Sorceress* and, as he reported to Madame von Meck, he dreamt 'of a time when I shall give concerts abroad'. Now that his fear of conducting in public had been conquered he was able to tell her that 'my nerves are much stronger, and things which formerly were not to be thought of, are now quite possible'. To prove the point he agreed to conduct a concert of his own works at St. Petersburg on 17 March 1887 where he received 'endless ovations'.

However, the score of *The Sorceress* was not finished until May of that year: 'the older I become, the more trouble my orchestration gives me'. On the completion of the new opera he embarked on his summer travels, calling first at Moscow for the Conservatoire examinations. From there he went on to Tiflis and then to Borzhom, accompanied by Modest, and Anatol and his wife. He was greatly impressed by the magnificent scenery in the Caucasus and devoted only one hour a day to his work, sketching a new string sextet and orchestrating a new orchestral suite — the 4th., which he entitled *Mozartiana*. His holiday was interrupted in July when he was summoned to Aachen, where his friend Nikolay Kondratyev lay dying. He made the journey with reluctance, feeling that he was acting not from kindness but from a sense of duty. Aachen itself did nothing to dispel his gloom:

I am now sitting here, and everyone admires my sacrifice. But there is no question of sacrifice. I lead a life of ease, gourmandise at the *table d'hote*, do nothing except spend my money on luxuries while others want for it for absolute necessities. Is not that real egoism? I do not act towards my neighbours as I should.

He put his time to good use, however, by completing the *Mozartiana* Suite and composing the *Pezzo Capriccioso* for 'cello and orchestra. He returned to Maidanovo in mid-September, and two weeks later he received news that Kondratyev had died. Deeply depressed, he filled his diary with philosophical ramblings:

How short life is! How much I still have to do, to think and to say! We keep putting things off and meanwhile death lurks round the corner.

In October rehearsals started for the première of *The Sorceress* at St. Petersburg. On 1 November, Tchaikovsky conducted the first performance, which was followed by four further presentations of the work. He was quite convinced that this was the best opera of his career and quite failed to notice a singular lack of enthusiasm on the part of his audiences. By the fifth performance the house was only half-filled, and not even Tchaikovsky could ignore the signs. He made his way back to Moscow miserable and much offended, complaining to Madame von Meck that he had never encountered 'such hatred and hostility' from the press:

Gabriel Fauré (1845-1924)

On no other opera have I expended so much labour and sacrifice: yet never before have I been so persecuted by the critics.

But within a matter of days the situation changed. In Moscow, he conducted a concert of his own music including the *1812 Overture* and a first performance of the *Mozartiana* Suite, to which his critics and the audience responded most generously. His confidence restored, Tchaikovsky laid plans for his first concert tour abroad: his international career was about to begin.

107

Chapter 10

Tchaikovsky on Tour

'Flashes of genius mingle with musical banalities' — Josef Sittard

Tchaikovsky's travels throughout Europe were no longer those of a nomad, for he had now an established base in his motherland Russia. When he embarked on his first major tour, on 27 December 1887, his first engagement was in Leipzig, but he took the opportunity of first visiting Berlin, where he was delighted to renew the acquaintance of the singer who had so infatuated him eighteen years earlier, Désirée Artôt. His host in Leipzig was Adolf Brodsky, and a fellow-guest was none other than Johannes Brahms. He described him as 'a handsome man, rather short and stout . . . his fine head, almost that of an old man, recalls the type of a handsome, benign, elderly Russian priest.' He clearly found him congenial company. Also staying at the Brodsky household were the Norwegian composer Grieg and his wife, and Tchaikovsky was delighted to find that his personality matched his 'warmly emotional music', which he had for so long admired. The distinguished English composer Dame Ethel Smyth was also a member of the party: Tchaikovsky described her as 'not handsome, but having what people call an expressive or an intelligent face'.

Early in the New Year, on 2 January 1888, Tchaikovsky faced his first test: an engagement to conduct the formidable Leipzig Gewandhaus Orchestra which was formed when Bach was a cantor at St. Thomas's School, and numbered among its distinguished conductors Felix Mendelssohn. Karl Reinecke (1860-1895) was the principal conductor during Tchaikovsky's visit, and he introduced the terrified composer to the orchestra at his first rehearsal. He responded with a brief, stammering speech in German, and managed to overcome his nervousness to such an extent that he was able to perform, quite successfully, his *First Suite* for orchestra. Brahms was in the audience, and Tchaikovsky confided to Modest that:

yesterday and today we have been a good deal together. We are ill at ease

Edvard Grieg (1843-1907)

because we do not really like each other, but he takes great pains to be kind to me.

Tchaikovsky admitted in his letter to feeling homesick already, and confessed that he found it all very tiring. Nevertheless, a public rehearsal on 4 January went extremely well, and the *First Suite* received a 'flattering ovation' from an audience which consisted, mainly of musicians and music students. Much to the composer's delight, Grieg sent him a note of warm congratulation and praise. The concert itself took place the following day and although it was not quite so successful, Tchaikovsky took two curtain calls. The critics were cautious, but expressed pleasant surprise that the work was not immediately identifiable as a product of the Russian school of 'storm and stress'. The following morning a Tchaikovsky festival was held at Liszt-Berein devoted to the composer's chamber music at which the piano trio was performed: this was greeted with unanimous praise from both audience and critics.

From Leipzig, Tchaikovsky travelled on to Hamburg where he heard an 'altered and aged' Hans von Bülow conduct an 'inspired' performance of Beethoven's 'Eroica' Symphony. With a few days

The Gewandhaus, Leipzig

The Railway Terminus in
Hamburg

Richard Strauss (1864-1949)

in hand, he decided to visit Lübeck where he saw a production of
Shakespeare's *Othello*, which he described as an 'agonising play'.
During his few days in the city he received a telegram from the
Director of the Imperial Opera, Vsevolozhsky, advising him that
the Tsar had granted him an annual pension of 3,000 roubles for
life. Doubting that he deserved such an honour, Tchaikovsky
returned to Hamburg to conduct a concert devoted entirely to his
own works including the First Piano Concerto and the *Serenade for
Strings*. The Hamburg audience was not impressed, and their reaction was more than adequately summed up in a review by Josef
Sittard which appeared in the *Hamburg Correspondent*:

We cannot deny to Tchaikovsky originality, temperament, or a bold
flight of fancy, although when he is possessed by the spirit of his race he
overthrows every limitation. All logic is then thrown to the winds, and
there begins a witches' Sabbath of sound which offends our sight and our
hearing, especially the latter. Flashes of genius mingle with musical
banalities . . .

The opinions of Sittard were echoed by the aged Chairman of the
Hamburg Philharmonic Society, Theodor Ave-Lallement,
although perhaps in a rather more amusing manner. He openly
admitted his dislike of Tchaikovsky's music, but he did see in him
the makings of a fine composer in the grand German tradition. As
Tchaikovsky later reported:

Almost with tears in his eyes he begged me to leave Russia and to settle
permanently in Germany where classical conventions and the traditions of

110

high culture could not fail but to correct my faults, which were easily explained by the fact of my having been born and educated in a country so unenlightened, and so far behind Germany.

Despite this frontal assault on his national pride Tchaikovsky and Ave-Lallement parted the best of friends. Later — and possibly with tongue in cheek — the composer dedicated his Fifth Symphony to him.

After Hamburg Tchaikovsky returned to Berlin where he gave a concert on 8 February: once again, the audience were far more enthusiastic than the critics, and Tchaikovsky was much offended by a suggestion that the house had been 'liberally papered'. It was on this occasion that he first heard the music of Richard Strauss, one of von Bülow's latest protégés, and he dismissed the Symphony, Op 12, as 'pretentious' and displaying 'an outstanding lack of talent'. Berlin was his last official engagement in Germany, but he paid a further brief visit to Leipzig before crossing the border into Bohemia, where he was scheduled to give a number of concerts in Prague.

In central Europe, political tension was running high. Bismarck had made a number of highly anti-Russian speeches, and

The Brandenburg Gate, Berlin

Prague about 1880

Tchaikovsky feared that his visit to Prague might be used as a propaganda weapon by the Czechs to stir up hatred against Germany herself. He expressed his concern to Madame von Meck, explaining that he had been very well treated in Germany and felt himself under a debt of obligation to the German people. While in Leipzig, a military band had serenaded him for a whole hour under his hotel window playing among other things, 'God Preserve the Tsar'. So the last thing he wanted was for the Czechs to use his visit for political ends.

His fears, however, were to prove quite groundless. On his arrival in Prague, the local people confined themselves to expressing their great admiration for, and devotion to, Russia, and the composer was fêted in a style usually reserved for royal visitors only. He soon found himself at the centre of a social whirlwind, involving many official engagements and an endless round of speech-making. His two concert performances were triumphs, and the great Czech composer Dvorak presented him with a score of his second Symphony which he inscribed 'To Peter Tchakiovsky, in memory of Prague: Antonin Dvorak, 18 February, 1888'. The Russian composer was astute enough to realise that the acclamation was not entirely the result of Czech admiration for him, or for his

112

Concert posters

Concert programs

music, as he noted in his diary after his first Prague concert:

> In general this is, of course, one of the most memorable days of my life. I have become very fond of these good Czechs — and with reason! Heaven! How much enthusiasm! And not for me really, but for dear Russia.

From Bohemia to France, where political overtones also played their part in the warmth of his reception. The Franco-Russian alliance had only just been concluded and all things Russian were greatly in vogue in the French capital at the time. He gave two concerts at the Châtelet to very enthusiastic audiences, although the critics suggested that he was not 'so Russian as people imagined' and took him to task for the length of his works. The final engagement of his tour was in London, where there were no political implications to his visit, and where he was allowed to spend four days more or less in his own company. His concert at the Royal Philharmonic Society, was a huge success. He conducted both the *Serenade for Strings* and the Variations from the *Third Suite* — performances which, it can truthfully be said, laid the foundations of his formidable reputation in Britain which has endured to the present day. His reception in London left him in an exultant mood but he was, nevertheless, relieved that his first international tour as a conductor had come to an end. He confided his thoughts in a letter to Jurgenson:

> I have expended a great deal of money and, even more, health and energy. In return I have gained some celebrity, but every hour I ask myself — why? Is it worthwhile? And I come to the conclusion that it is far better to live quietly, without fame.

Antonin Dvorak (1841-1904)

While Tchaikovsky was away on tour his manservant, Alexey Sofronov, had carried out his instructions to move into a new country house at Frolovskoye, just outside Klin. Pausing only for a brief stay at Tiflis, Tchaikovsky took possession of his new home in April 1888. It was 'simpler and not so well furnished as Maidanovo', but it stood in a picturesque setting on a wooded hill. A month later, Tchaikovsky wrote to Modest saying that he had 'fallen in love' with his new house, and described it as 'paradise':

> It is indeed so beautiful that when I go out for a half-hour walk in the morning, I feel compelled to extend it to two hours . . . I have not yet begun work apart from a few corrections. To speak frankly, I feel as yet no impulse for creative work . . . Have I written myself out? No ideas — no inclination?

113

In similar vein, he told Madame von Meck that he was content to cultivate his garden: '. . . just now I am busy with flowers and with flower-growing'. However, by 22 June the creative urge had returned, and in a subsequent letter he told her that:

I am dreadfully anxious to prove, not only to others but also to myself, that I am not yet *played out* as a composer. Have I already told you that I intend to write a symphony? The beginning was difficult: now, however, inspiration seems to have come. We shall see!

His inspiration bore fruit as the Fifth Symphony in E minor, which he completed very rapidly, by the end of August. He considered it 'thank God, no worse than the others', and followed it up at once by writing the Fantasy Overture *Hamlet*, which he dedicated to Grieg. Both these new works received their first performances in St. Petersburg: Tchaikovsky conducted on both occasions. The new symphony was performed on 17 November, and *Hamlet* a week later on 24 November, at which concert the symphony was given a repeat performance. Both concerts failed miserably.

A flying visit to Prague to conduct *Eugene Onegin*, the Fifth Symphony and the Second Piano Concerto offered no consolation, as the concerts were poorly attended as a result of incompetent management. Back in Frolovskoye, Tchaikovsky's depression deepened when he heard the news of the deaths of two people close to him — his old friend Hubert, and Vera Davidov. Not for the first time in his career, he completely lost confidence in a major work, as this letter to Madame von Meck reveals:

After two performances of my new Symphony in Petersburg, and one in

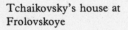

Tchaikovsky's house at Frolovskoye

114

Tchaikovsky in 1888

Prague, I have come to the conclusion that it is a failure. There is something repellent, something superfluous, patchy and insincere, which the public instinctively recognises . . . The consciousness of this brings me a sharp twinge of self-dissatisfaction. Am I really played out, as they say? Can I merely repeat and ring the changes on my earlier idiom? Last night I looked through *our* Symphony (No.4). What a difference! How immeasurably superior it is! It is very, very sad.

As we now know, this unfavourable comparison between the Fifth Symphony and its immediate predecessor was, to say the least, premature, and it is perhaps a matter of some satisfaction that Tchaikovsky lived long enough to see his judgement reversed by the great popular success which the later work came to enjoy. At the time, however, he returned to his desk for consolation, and buried himself in preparatory sketches for a new ballet *The Sleeping*

115

Beauty which had been suggested to him by Vsevolozhsky. Within five weeks the first four scenes were complete, and on 2 February preliminary rehearsals were started at the Bolshoi. Three days later Tchaikovsky left on his second international tour as a conductor which, once again, was to begin in Germany.

He made his début in Cologne on 12 February, conducting the *Third Suite*. Already he had written to Modest that he was 'seized' by homesickness and a longing to return home, but the concert was a triumph. The orchestra played a fanfare when he was recalled to

Page from the manuscript
of the Fifth Symphony
(Third movement: Valse)

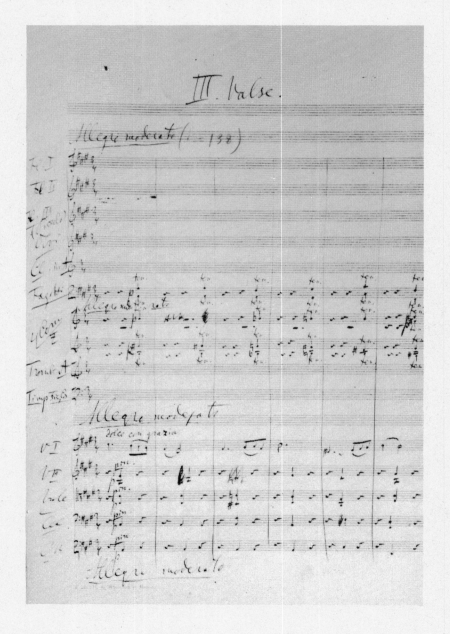

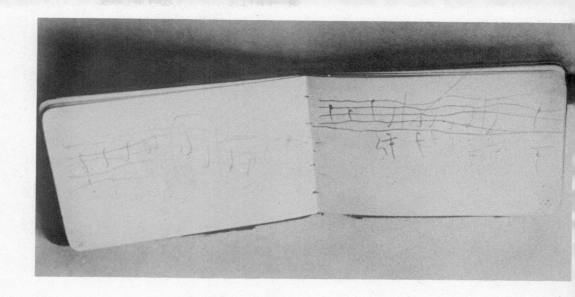

Notebook showing Tchaikovsky's plans for the Fifth Symphony

Tchaikovsky in 1890

V. Brianza, first performer as Princess Aurora
in *The Sleeping Beauty*

Scene from *The Sleeping Beauty* in first performance at the Marinski Theatre in St. Petersburg, 189[

Dr Johannes Brahms (1833-97)
an early photograph

the platform to receive his ovation. Frankfurt proved no less successful even though, as he pointed out to Glazunov, 'the Frankfurt public is very classical, and I am regarded in Germany as a notorious revolutionary'. By comparison, his concert in Dresden was a failure, for which he blamed the 'third-rate' orchestra that had found the Fourth Symphony, technically, too demanding. Exhausted, he arrived in Berlin where his appearance was greeted by a mixture of applause and hissing. Geneva proved a great success, and he was presented with a gilt laurel-wreath by the Russian community. On 11 March he arrived in Hamburg for his last concert in Germany, and was flattered to learn that Brahms had extended his visit there to attend the rehearsal of the Fifth Symphony. At lunch afterwards, Brahms gave his 'frank' opinion of the work, finding it enjoyable apart from the finale. Tchaikovsky, was impressed by his honesty, and responded by inviting Brahms to visit Moscow to conduct a Russian Musical Society concert — an invitation which was politely turned down. At the concert on 15 March, the Symphony was 'magnificently played' and enthusiastically received, which made Tchaikovsky change his opinion of the work — 'I like it far better now'. Poor Ave-Lallement had been too ill to hear the work dedicated to him. The triumph in Hamburg and elsewhere were marred for Tchaikovsky

117

by the lack of interest of the Russian press: 'With the exception of my nearest and dearest', he wrote to Bob Davidov, 'no one will ever hear of my successes. In the daily papers here one reads long telegrams about Wagner's performances in Russia. Certainly I am not a second Wagner, but it would be desirable for Russia to learn how I have been received in Germany.'

On 8 March he arrived in Paris, and with almost a month to wait until his last engagement in London he spent his time visiting friends and attending the opera. He heard Colonne perform three movements from the *Third Suite* which, much to his satisfaction, was a splendid success. Arriving in London, he was impressed as much by the fog as by the standard of the orchestra — 'I never dreamt of anything like the one we had today'. His concerts, promoted by the London Philharmonic Society at the St James's Hall, confirmed the reputation he had gained the previous year. On 12 April, claiming to Bob Davidov that he would never leave Frolovskoye again, he began his homeward journey, making first for Marseilles, where he took a steamer through the Mediterranean to Batum, and then onwards to Tiflis and Moscow, arriving there on 19 May.

Relieved to be home he happily settled in Frolovskoye, where he spent the summer months hard at work on *The Sleeping Beauty*. The new ballet proved difficult. 'The instrumentation gives me more trouble than it used to', he wrote to Nadezhda von Meck on 6 August, 'consequently the work goes slowly, but perhaps all the better. Many of my earlier compositions show traces of hurry and lack of thought'. By the end of the month the score was complete, and Tchaikovsky spent the autumn months of 1889 fulfilling conducting engagements, which included the Moscow revival of *Eugene Onegin* and a performance of Beethoven's Ninth Symphony. During December he agreed to conduct three works by Anton Rubinstein; *Conzertstück*, the Symphonic poem *Russia* and the oratorio *The Tower of Babel*. The concerts were part of Rubinstein's jubilee celebrations and afterwards Tchaikovsky admitted to having gone 'through a martyrdom'.

Meanwhile rehearsals for *The Sleeping Beauty* progressed, and on 14 January 1890 Tsar Alexander III was present at a gala performance. To Tchaikovsky's chagrin, the Tsar could only muster up enough enthusiasm to comment 'very nice' at the end of the performance: in his diary, Tchaikovsky wrote: 'His Majesty treated me in a most offhand manner, God be with him.' In truth, he had expected the new ballet to be an outstanding success. He personally regarded the music as some of his best, the production was the most sumptuous ever seen in Russia and the choreography, by Marius Petipa, he considered brilliant. To his bitter disappointment, the public's response was no more encouraging than the Tsar's, and in

'Puss in Boots' from 'The Sleeping Beauty'

The 'beloved' nephew 'Bob'
Davidov

desperation Tchaikovsky escaped to Western Europe. Only when
he arrived in Berlin did he choose his final destination: Florence.

He had not visited the Italian city for eight years, and soon after
his arrival there on 30 January he immersed himself in work on a
new opera *The Queen of Spades*. Three years earlier Modest had
prepared a libretto based on Pushkin's story for the composer
Klenovsky, who had rejected it. When Vsevolozhsky suggested the
same subject, Tchaikovsky had submitted his brother's libretto for
approval which it received. The more Tchaikovsky wrote of the
score, the greater his enthusiasm became, and he bombarded
Modest with demands for revisions. By 31 March he had
completed the piano arrangement of Act II, and solemnly informed
his brother that, 'either I am greatly mistaken or *The Queen of
Spades* is a masterpiece'. A week later he moved on to Rome, and

119

the following day the piano arrangement of the entire opera was finished: by the time he arrived home in Frolovskoye at the beginning of May, Act I was orchestrated. His homecoming was ruined by changes that had taken place at his absence, 'the whole — literally every stick — of the forest, has been cut down.' Despite his disappointment, on 5 June he was able to note in his diary, 'end of opera'. Immediately he began sketching a string sextet *Souvenir de Florence* Op 70, which he completed by the end of the month with 'the greatest enthusiasm and without the least exertion'. The music reflected the general cheerfulness of his mood, and in August he visited Alexandra at Kamenka, but sensing that an atmosphere of gloom now pervaded the house due to his sister's illness, he moved on to Tiflis to stay with Anatol and his wife.

Then, on 4 October he received a letter from Nadezhda von Meck in which she claimed to be on the brink of bankruptcy. She told him that his allowance must stop and the end of the letter hinted that it was also the end of their friendship: 'Do not forget, and think of me sometimes'. Tchaikovsky replied the same day:

'Dearest Friend, — The news you communicated to me in your last letter caused me great anxiety; not on my account, however, but on your own. It would, of course, be untrue were I to say that such a radical change in my budget did not in any way affect my financial position. But it ought not to affect me so seriously as you apparently fear. In recent years my earnings have considerably increased, and there are indications that they will continue to do so. Therefore, if I am accountable for any fraction of your endless cares and anxieties, I beg you, for God's sake, to be assured that I can think of this pecuniary loss without any bitterness. Believe me, this is the simple truth; I am no master of empty phraseology. That I shall have to economise a little is of no importance. What really matters is that you, with your requirements and large ways of life, should have to retrench. This is terribly hard and vexatious. I feel as though I wanted to lay the blame on someone (you yourself are certainly above reproach), but I do not know who is the real culprit. Besides, not only is my indignation quite useless, but I have no right to interfere in your family affairs. I would rather ask Ladislaw Pakhulsky to tell me what you intend to do, where you will live, and how far you will be straitened as to means. I cannot think of you except as a wealthy woman. The last words of your letter have hurt me a little, but I do not think you meant them seriously. Do you really think me incapable of remembering you when I no longer receive your money? How could I forget for a moment all you have done for me, and all for which I owe you gratitude? I may say without exaggeration that you saved me. I should certainly have gone out of my mind and come to an untimely end but for your friendship and sympathy, as well as for the material assistance (then my safety anchor), which enabled me to rally my forces and take up once more my chosen vocation. No, dear friend, I shall always remember and bless you with my last breath. I am glad you can now no longer spend your means upon me, so that I may show my unbounded and passionate gratitude, which passes all words. Perhaps you yourself hardly suspect how immeasurable has been your generosity. If you did, you would never have said that, now you are poor, I am to think of you *'sometimes'*. I can truly say that I have never forgotten you, and never shall forget you for a moment, for whenever I think of myself my thoughts turn directly to you.

'I kiss your hands, with all my heart's warmth, and implore you to believe, once and for all, that no one feels more keenly for your troubles than I do.

'I will write another time about myself and all I am doing. Forgive my hasty, badly written letter: I am too much upset to write well.'

Tchaikovsky's letter was never answered. Shortly afterwards he learned that Madame von Meck's financial difficulties had been resolved and that there was no question of her being declared bankrupt. His relief of hearing the news gave way, not unnaturally, to a feeling of resentment, mortification and wounded pride. Try as he might, he could not banish from his mind a suspicion that Madame von Meck's last letter was merely 'an excuse to get rid of him at the earliest opportunity'. He determined to unearth the truth behind this bizarre end to a bizarre friendship.

121

Chapter 11

America

'What I need is to believe in myself again, for my faith in myself is shattered and it seems to me that my rôle is ended' — Tchaikovsky

Tchaikovsky's reassuring words to Madame von Meck that her decision would not affect him 'so seriously as you apparently fear' were not echoed in a letter he sent shortly afterwards to Jurgenson:

Now I must start quite a fresh life, on a totally different scale of expenditure. In all possibility I shall be compelled to seek some occupation in St. Petersburg which will bring me in a good salary. This is very, very humiliating — yes: humiliating is the word.

When he subsequently heard that his benefactress was not bankrupt, he wrote to his publisher again:

Such were my relations with her that I never felt oppressed by her generous gifts, but now they weigh upon me in retrospect. My pride is hurt; my faith in her unfailing readiness to help me and make any sacrifice for my sake, is betrayed.

Here we have the crux of the matter: it was the composer's pride which suffered more than his pocket as a result of Madame von Meck's seemingly brutal action. He wrote further letters to her, assuring her of his continued friendship and affection and seeking from her some explanation. These, too, received no answer and in desperation he wrote to Madame von Meck's son-in-law, Pakhulsky, who politely replied to the effect that she was too ill and 'nervously upset' to write. There is other, quite independent, evidence to show that Nadezhda Filaretovna was indeed the victim of an extreme nervous disorder 'which changed her relations not only to Tchaikovsky, but to others'. On 18 June 1891, the composer sought Pakhulsky's help once more in an effort to discover the truth and to re-kindle the long friendship, and asked him to deliver

Tchaikovsky in 1891

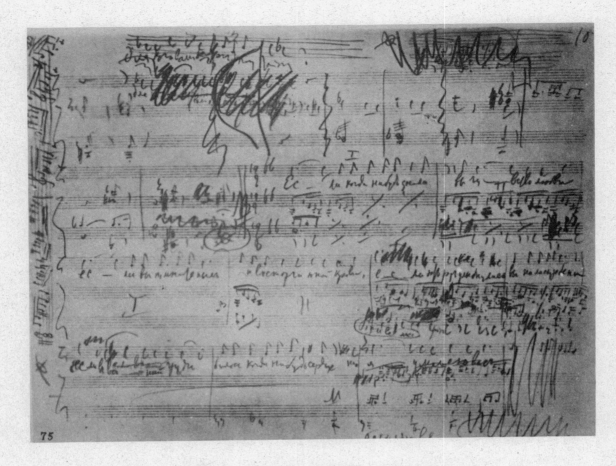

Autograph of sketch for the opera *Queen of Spades*

Scene from *Queen of Spades* in first performance at the Marinski Theatre in St. Petersburg, 1890

a letter personally to Madame von Meck. Pakhulsky refused and the letter was returned.

Tchaikovsky made no further attempt to solve the riddle. His attitude became curiously ambivalent: on the one hand, he retained his affection for Madame von Meck to the end, and his sorrow at the rift which had so unexpectedly occurred was genuine and profound. On the other hand, he started to make slighting references to the relationship: he called it a 'commonplace, silly joke' which filled him with 'disgust and shame'. 'The old, ideal friendship' as M. D. Calvocoressi puts it, 'now appeared to him as the mere caprice of a wealthy woman . . . Her last letter rankled in his heart to the end of his days.' One of the many possible explanations put forward for her apparent heartlessness is that someone close to her, possibly her daughter Julia, unveiled Tchaikovsky's mask of conventional respectability and revealed his true homosexual nature. There is no evidence to support this conjecture and, indeed, it seems unlikely in view of the fact some of the early letters from Madame von Meck suggest that she was not only aware of Tchaikovsky's sexual preferences, but also understood them. Pakhulsky's explanation that his mother-in-law was suffering from a severe nervous disorder seems much more likely. In any event, it was the only explanation which was offered to Tchaikovsky and, like the composer, we have little alternative but to accept it.

The première of *The Queen of Spades* on 19 December 1890 in St. Petersburg, under Napravnik, gave Tchaikovsky some consolation. The opera was an instant success with the public: two days earlier it had received the seal of Imperial approval when the Tsar attended the dress rehearsal. Modest recalls that 'throughout the entire even-

A scene from 'The Nutcracker'

123

Tchaikovsky and Bob
Davidov

ing, artists and audience alike experienced a sense of complete satisfaction rarely felt during any operatic performance'. The public's
enthusiasm, however, was not mirrored in the press, which
published consistently unfavourable reviews. One critic went so far
as to remark that 'not only does Tchaikovsky repeat himself, but he
does not shrink from imitating other composers'. A few days later
the opera was mounted in Kiev, where the public's enthusiasm was
even greater than at St. Petersburg.

Tchaikovsky, who was present, received a rapturous reception.
From this triumph in Kiev he travelled to Kamenka to celebrate
the new year, anxiously searching for subjects for a new opera and
ballet which the Opera Directorate had commissioned for the forthcoming season. He asked Modest to consider Hanrik Hertz's *King
René's Daughter* as a possible source for the opera, adding that he
would most probably go to Italy to compose it.

124

Modest Tchaikovsky, brother and biographer of Peter
and writer of libretto for *Queen of Spades*

Portrayal of the old countess in a Paris National Opera
rendition of *Queen of Spades*

Stage decoration for first performance of *The Nutcracker*

Scene from *The Nutcracker* as performed at the Bolshoi Theatre in Moscow, 1940

Returning to Frolovskoye on 18 January 1891 he busied himself with an uncongenial task, composing incidental music to *Hamlet*, which he had promised the French actor Lucien Guitry for a benefit performance in February. Most of the music consisted of arrangements of earlier pieces, using a great deal of material from the Fantasy Overture *Hamlet*, the *alla tedesca* of the Third Symphony and the incidental music to *The Snow Maiden*. But there were some original items, among them the popular *Funeral March*. With the promise to Guitry honoured, he settled down to sketching out a new ballet, the subject of which had been dictated to him by the Opera Directorate. The story of *The Nutcracker*, a version by Dumas of Hoffman's fairy-tale *The Nutcracker and the King of the Mice* left Tchaikovsky thoroughly indifferent, but as work progressed he became more enthusiastic. He was anxious to complete as much of the work as possible before setting out on his most ambitious foreign tour yet, which, at the invitation of Walter Damrosch, would take him across the Atlantic to America for the first time. During March he left Frolovskoye and, after preliminary discussions with Petipa in St. Petersburg about the staging of *The Nutcracker*, set out for Western Europe on 18 March.

Work continued on the new ballet en route to Berlin, where he attended a performance of the *1812* Overture and wrote to Bob Davidov, describing his pleasure at sitting 'incognito among a strange audience' listening to his own music. The letter also gave his remedy for the 'agonizing homesickness' which was already attacking him — 'intoxication'. From Berlin he made his way to Paris where he was to conduct a Colonne concert of his own works. Fortunately, Modest, Sapelnikov and Sophie Menter were also there, as he had become increasingly depressed and homesick. Even the success of the concert did not brighten his spirits and, to make matters worse, he still had twelve days to wait before sailing from

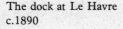

The dock at Le Havre
c.1890

The Tower of Joan of Arc,
Rouen

Le Havre. In an attempt to kill time and to work on *The Nutcracker*, Tchaikovsky decided to spend ten days in Rouen, and it was arranged that Modest, Sapelinkov and Sophie Menter should meet him there on 16 April, and bid him farewell from Le Havre the following day. The plans fell through, for on 9 April Modest received news that their beloved sister Alexandra had died. Realizing the shattering effect the tragic news would have on his brother, he travelled alone to Rouen the following day to break it personally. He found Tchaikovsky extremely depressed and lonely, but so delighted to see him that Modest decided it wiser to allow him to cross the Atlantic in ignorance of Alexandra's death. There, he reasoned, many diversions would help to soften the blow. Making the excuse that homesickness was driving him home earlier than he had planned, Modest left for St. Petersburg happy in the belief that he had spared his brother unnecessary suffering. His well-intentioned action, however, failed. Tchaikovsky's depression became so acute that in desperation he returned to Paris and, by chance, picked up a Russian newspaper in the reading room of the Passage de l'Opéra. It contained the announcement of Alexandra's death. He wrote Modest:

I ran out as though stung by a snake. Later I went to Sophie Menter's and Sapelnikov's. What a fortunate thing they were here . . . At first I thought it my duty to abandon America and go to Petersburg, but afterwards I realized this would be useless. I should have to return the 5,000 francs I had received, relinquish the rest and lose my ticket. No, I must go to America. Mentally I am suffering a great deal. I am very anxious about Bob [Davidov], although I know from my own experience that at his age we easily recover from such blows . . . For God's sake write all details to New York. Today, even more than yesterday, I feel the absolute impossibility of depicting in music the Sugar-plum Fairy.

Gloomily Tchaikovsky set sail for America. The suicide of a fellow-passenger during the first hours at sea and violent sea-sickness increased his depression. He was thankful when they neared America — 'I simply couldn't bear to stay on board ship any longer' — but on arriving in New York he was furious to learn that the visit had been extended to take in Philadelphia and Baltimore without his consent. He spent his first night in New York crying in his hotel room, though he did venture out on to Broadway, which he described to Modest as 'an extraordinary street! Houses of one and two stories alternate with some nine-storied buildings. Most original! I was struck with the number of nigger faces I saw'. Early misgivings soon disappeared with the overwhelming display of American hospitality which he received. The four New York

concerts in which he appeared were part of the inaugural celebra-
tions for the opening of the New York Music Hall (now the
Carnegie Hall), and each was a personal triumph. In a letter to Bob
Davidov on 30 April he happily observed that

I am convinced that I am ten times more famous in America than in
Europe. At first when others spoke to me about it, I thought it only their
exaggerated kindness. But now I see it is really so. Several of my works
which are unknown even in Moscow, are frequently played here. I am a
much more important person here than in Russia. Is it not curious?'

The concerts in Baltimore and Philadelphia confirmed his

A contemporary scene of
Broadway

The steps of the Capitol in
Washington (c.1890)

popularity, and a brief visit to Washington prompted the Russian
Embasy there to arrange a musical evening in tribute to their
eminent compatriot. On the eve of his departure from America,
Tchaikovsky attended a farewell party arranged for him by the
Composers' Club at the Metropolitan Opera. The following day,
20 May, he set sail for Europe, exhausted, but well-satisfied by his
triumphant American visit. By the end of the month he was back in

Tchaikovsky in 1892

Drawing of a celeste

Tchaikovsky with Alexander Siloti

St. Petersburg, happy to be once again amongst his family and friends.

During his absence, Alexey Sofronov had moved back to Maidanovo, since Frolovskoye with its treeless scenery had lost all charm for Tchaikovsky. Although the house at Maidanovo was showing signs of decay, he was able to resume work on *The Nutcracker*. While in Paris, he had discovered a new instrument invented by Vicor Mustel, the *Celeste* '. . . something between a piano and a *glockenspiel*, with a heavenly tone' — and on 15 June he informed Jurgenson of his intention to include it in the score of the new ballet. 'Have it sent direct to St. Petersburg', he added, 'but no one there must know about it. I am afraid Rimsky-Korsakov and Glazunov might hear of it and make use of the effect before I could. I expect the instrument will make a tremendous sensation'. The sketches of the ballet were completed by 7 July, but Tchaikovsky was unenthusiastic about them. He wrote to Bob Davidov:

It is far weaker than *The Sleeping Beauty*: the old fellow is getting worn out . . . Not only is his hair turning white as snow and beginning to fall, not only is he losing his teeth, not only do his eyes grow weaker and get tired sooner, not only do his feet begin to drag — but he is growing less capable of accomplishing anything.

It is true that at fifty he looked older than his years, but his hypochondria would appear to have coloured this self-portrait into lurid fantasy. His physical ailments, however, did not prevent him from beginning work on the new opera, based on *King René's Daughter*, as he had proposed. But now it had a new title, *Iolanthe*. By mid-September the sketch was complete, and he turned his attention to the composition of a large-scale orchestral tone-poem *The Voyevoda*, which he conducted for the first time at a Siloti concert in Moscow on 18 November. During rehearsals Tchaikovsky had been upset by his friends comparing it unfavourably with *Romeo and Juliet* and *Francesca da Rimini*. He conducted the work with complete indifference, and during the interval threatened to destroy the score declaring that 'such rubbish should never have been written'. The following day he carried out his threat, but fortunately Siloti had taken the precaution of hiding a set of orchestral parts. *The Voyevoda* was later reconstructed and published posthumously as Opus 78.

Tchaikovsky found consolation in scoring *Iolanthe*, which he completed by the end of December. Immediately he set out on another concert tour of Western Europe, first visiting Kiev to conduct two concerts of his own music and, after pausing briefly at Kamenka, where, Modest recalls, 'a feeling of sadness came over

The Church of the Holy
Cross, Warsaw, with the
University in the
background (1889)

him at the sight of his old dwelling place, so inseparably connected
with the memory of the sister he had lost', he arrived in Warsaw on
10 January 1892. In spite of the 'worse than second-rate' orchestra,
his concert there four days later was a triumph, and he was fêted by
everyone, including a number of Polish countesses whom he
described as 'fascinatingly amiable'. Inevitably, his enjoyment was
marred by attacks of homesickness, and he wrote despairing letters
to Bob Davidov about 'counting the days, hours and minutes'
before he could return to his beloved Russia.

From Warsaw he travelled on to Hamburg, where he conducted a
performance of *Eugene Onegin*. He was impressed to find the
singers and orchestra well-prepared, but the translation from
Russian to German had necessitated minor alterations in the score.
These he failed to master and in exasperation he handed over the
baton to the local conductor, Gustav Mahler. 'The conductor here
is not merely passable', he informed his nephew, 'but actually has
genius'. The opera, as he had predicted, was not well-received, but
he considered its performance as 'positively superb'. Within a few
days he arrived in Paris, deeply depressed, homesick, and in two
minds whether or not to abandon his scheduled concerts in Holland
and to return home. Ten days later he made his decision and
returned to Maidanovo.

130

His most pressing task was to arrange parts of *The Nutcracker* into a suite, which would replace the ill-fated *Voyevoda* at a concert in St. Petersburg on 7 March. *The Nutcracker* Suite was greeted with tremendous applause, and five of its six movements had to be repeated. Two weeks later the entire ballet was complete, and Tchaikovsky left for Moscow to fulfil three conducting engagements: Gounod's *Faust*, Rubinstein's *The Demon* and his own *Eugene Onegin*. So popular was he with the opera company, that on his departure from the station on 17 May the entire orchestra and singers turned out to bid him farewell. He was making for the new country house Alexey Sofronov had prepared at Klin. Although his new residence had only a small garden and ordinary views, its one great advantage was the size of its rooms, which were unusually large for a small country house in Russia. Klin was to be Tchaikovsky's last home. After his death it was purchased by Alexey Sofronov, who passed it on to Modest and Bob Davidov in 1897, and it later became the Tchaikovsky Museum. The State eventually took possession, and was responsible for the complete restoration of the house after it was ransacked by German armies in 1941.

No sooner had Tchaikovsky settled at Klin and had begun sketches for a new symphony, his growing restlessness and 'catarrh of the stomach' made him take flight to Western Europe, this time in the company of Bob Davidov, to take a water cure at Vichy.

House at Klin

131

The plaque on the door of the house at Klin which reads:
P. I. Tchaikovsky
At home Mondays and Thursdays
3-5 pm
NOT IN Please do not ring

Returning to Klin at the end of July, he resumed work on the new symphony in E flat. Much of his time was also spent correcting and editing proofs of new editions of his works. The symphony made little progress and he wrote Jurgenson that he had 'no time for it'. He had great hopes for a concert he was to conduct in Vienna as part of an Exhibition for music and theatre: 'So far Vienna has been hostile to me. I should like to overcome this unfriendly opinion'. But when he arrived in Vienna on 18 September, he discovered that he was to conduct a useless orchestra in what appeared to be no more than a beer-cellar. Horrified, he fled with Sophie Menter and Sapelnikov to her castle at Ilter in the Tyrol — 'peace and stillness, and not a trace of any other visitors'. On his homeward journey he attended the première of *The Queen of Spades* in Prague, which caused a sensation. Back in Russia, he was confronted with endless official duties, concerts to attend and the one-hundredth performance of *Eugene Onegin* at the Maryinsky Theatre ('the beloved composer was greeted with stormy ovations and presented with a wreath' reported the *Moskovskiye Vyedomosti*) all of which he found increasingly irksome. Now that he had attained the position of Russia's foremost composer, he was in no mood to enjoy it. Rehearsals for *Iolanthe* and *The Nutcracker*, which were to be given their first performances in a double bill, had begun and Tchaikovsky arrived in St. Petersburg at the beginning of

Tchaikovsky's grand piano at Klin

A corner of the study

November to supervise them. On 17 December Tsar Alexander III attended the premières 'full of compliments'. However, neither work was a success: the critics were united in their dislike and on 22 December Tchaikovsky wrote to Anatol that he was in 'a hateful frame of mind' after four days of all the papers 'cutting up both my creations'. A few months later he did admit that the ballet 'was a little boring, despite the magnificence of the setting'. Both works fell into neglect, a state from which *Iolanthe* has not emerged.

With the double failure, Tchaikovsky escaped once more to Western Europe. Modest remarks that 'it seemed as though he had become the victim of some blind force which drove him hither and thither at will . . . He could not remain long in one spot; but this was chiefly because it always seemed to him that "every place is better than the one which we are in" . . . His death, which came as a solution to the problem, seemed fortuitous. Yet it is clear to me that it came at a moment *'when things could not have gone on much longer'*. Indeed, if Tchaikovsky expected to find consolation in Western Europe, he was sadly mistaken. From Berlin on 28

December he wrote Bob Davidov of his intention to abandon the new symphony — 'the work is written for the sake of writing, and is not interesting or moving . . . Am I done for and dried up?' From Basle a few days later, he wrote to Modest that he had no news, except for 'fits of weeping' and that the following day he was going to Montbeillard to visit Fanny Durbach, his beloved governess of forty years earlier, who he had only recently discovered was still living. The prospect filled him with 'morbid fear and horror, as though I were entering the kingdom of the dead and the world of those who had long since vanished'. He was relieved to find her hardly changed, and not looking her seventy years:

I had dreaded tears and an affecting scene, but . . . she greeted me as though we had not met for a year — joyfully and tenderly, but quite simply . . . the past rose up so clearly before me that I seemed to inhale the air of Votinsk and hear my mother's voice distinctly.

After a fond farewell, Tchaikovsky travelled on to Paris and then to Brussels on 14 January. Ten days later he was in Odessa, supervising rehearsals for *The Queen of Spades* and conducting a series of

Tchaikovsky's desk

Kuznetsov's famous portrait of Tchaikovsky (1893) 'no truer, more living likeness of him exists' *Modest Tchaikovsky*

all-Tchaikovsky concerts. He also found time to sit for the famous portrait by Kuznetsov, about which Modest writes:

> Although the artist knew nothing of Tchaikovsky's inner life he has succeeded . . . in divining all the tragedy of that mental and spiritual phase through which the composer was passing at that time . . . no truer, more living likeness of him exists.

In a state of utter exhaustion from the frenzied activity of previous months, Tchaikovsky returned to Klin at the beginning of February 1893 convinced that there was no future for him. 'What I need is to believe in myself again', he wrote to Modest on 9 February 'for my faith in myself is shattered, and it seems to me that my rôle is ended.'

* * *

One week later he started work on a new symphony. It was a work which was to prove to him that his rôle had by no means ended. To the world it was to prove to be his masterpiece.

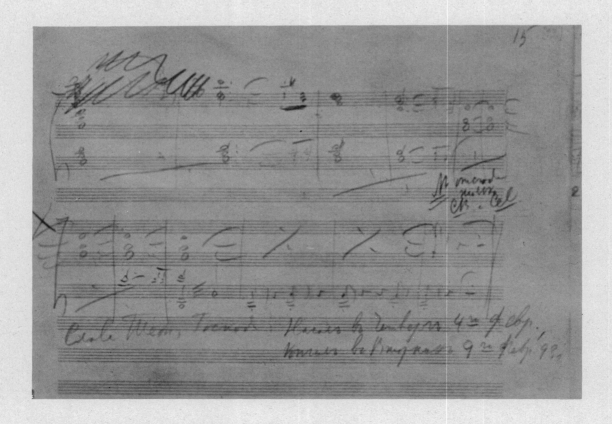

Autograph of sketch for the Sixth Symphony

Tchaikovsky in his latter years

Tchaikovsky in the garden of his country house at Klin

Chapter 12

Peace

'On my word of honour, I have never felt such self-satisfaction, such pride, such happiness, as in the knowledge that I have created a good thing' — Tchaikovsky

The first mention we have of a sixth symphony is in a letter which Tchaikovsky wrote to his nephew, Bob Davidov, on 23 February 1893:

As you know, I destroyed a symphony which I had partly composed and orchestrated in the autumn. I acted wisely for it contained little that was really fine — an empty pattern of sounds without any inspiration. Just as I was starting on my journey (the visit to Paris in December 1892) the idea came to me for a new symphony. This time with a programme; but a programme of the kind that will remain an enigma to all — let them guess it who can. The work will be entitled "A Programme Symphony" (No. 6). This programme is filled with subjective feelings. During my journey, while composing it in my mind, I frequently shed tears. Now I am home again I have settled down to sketch out the work, and it goes with such ardour that in less than four days I have completed the first movement, while the rest of the Symphony is clearly outlined in my head. There will be much in this work that is novel as regards form. For instance, the Finale will not be a great allegro, but an Adagio of considerable dimensions. You cannot imagine what joy I feel at the knowledge that my day is not yet over, and that I may still accomplish much. Perhaps I am mistaken, but it does not seem likely.

Apart from engagements during March, one in Kharkov and the other in Moscow, Tchaikovsky was able to work on his new symphony without interruption, with the result that sketches for the complete work were ready by 15 April — a remarkably short space of time. At that point he set the manuscript aside in order to fulfil a commission from Jurgenson for as many songs and piano pieces 'as he cared to write'. This project also went well, as we learn from a later letter to Bob Davidov:

I am engaged in making musical pancakes, and today I tossed the tenth. It is remarkable — the more I do, the easier and more pleasant the occupa-

Tchaikovsky in 1891

137

The Bolshoi Theatre,
Moscow

Sergei Rachmaninoff
(1873-1943)

tion becomes . . . If I could spend a whole year in the country and if my publisher were prepared to take everything I composed, I might make about 36,000 roubles a year.

The results of all this creative endeavour were the *Eighteen Piano Pieces* Op 72; a set of six songs — among the finest he ever composed — which are settings of poems by Dimitry Rathaus and published as Op 73; a *Military March* which he wrote as a special favour for his cousin Andrey Tchaikovsky, who was colonel of an infantry regiment, and a transcription of Mozart's Piano Fantasy No. 4, for four voices and piano.

On 9 May 1893 he attended the opening night, at the Bolshoi, of an opera entitled *Aleko* written by a nineteen-year-old student, Sergei Rachmaninoff. He was considerably impressed by the work of this unknown young man who, in many ways, was destined to become his natural successor in the authentic Russian tradition. Towards the end of May he arrived in London where two concerts had been arranged by the London Philharmonic Society at which works by a number of foreign composers, all of whom were due to receive honorary degrees at Cambridge, were to be performed. It had been a good year so far for the composer, but by the time he reached London his old enemies — nostalgia, homesickness and restlessness — had returned as this letter, also to Bob Davidov, reveals:

138

Is it not strange that I elected to undergo this torture of my own free will? What devil can have suggested it to me? Several times during my journey yesterday I resolved to throw in the whole thing and turn tail. But what a disgrace to turn back for no good reason! Yesterday I suffered so much that I could neither sleep nor eat, which is very unusual for me. I suffer not only from torments that cannot be put into words (there is a place in my new symphony — the sixth — where they seem to be adequately expressed), but from a dislike of strangers and an indefinable terror — though of what, the devil only knows.

His letter goes on to complain of internal pains and weakness in the legs, and the composer vows that he will never again undertake a foreign trip except for 'a heap of money'. On 1 June he conducted a performance of his fourth symphony, the work by which he had chosen to be represented, to an enthralled London audience. Two days later he proudly reported to Modest that his first concert 'had been a brilliant success. It was unanimously agreed that I scored a real triumph, so much so that Saint-Saëns, who followed me, suffered somewhat as a result.' It is clear that this success dispersed his gloom, if only for a short time, for he admitted that his initial impression of London had been greatly influenced by the bad weather —

Hyde Park in London
(c.1890)

so that I got no idea of what the town is really like. The devil knows Paris is a mere village compared with London! Walking in Regent Street or in Hyde Park one sees so many carriages, such splendid and luxurious *equipages*, that the eye is fairly dazzled.

However, a week later his mood of depression had returned: we find him complaining about the 'infernal life' he had to lead 'without a moment's peace', and of his 'perpetual agitation, dread, homesickness and fatigue'. He consoles himself with the thought that 'the hour of escape is at hand'.

The hour of escape was presumably the start of the ceremonies at Cambridge where, on 12 June, he presented himself together with Saint-Saëns, Boito and Max Bruch. Grieg was also to have been honoured but he was, unfortunately, too ill to attend the ceremony. Saint-Saëns was, of course, an old friend and he got on reasonably well with Boito: Max Bruch, on the other hand, he found 'an un-sympathetic, inflated sort of personage.' That evening a concert was given at which each of the composers conducted one of his own works. For this occasion Tchaikovsky chose his symphonic poem *Francesca da Rimini*, which prompted Saint-Saëns to pay tribute to his 'great talent and astounding technique'. The following

A contemporary scene of the market place in Cambridge

140

Max Bruch (1838-1920)

Arrigo Boito (1842-1918)

morning, the four composers 'dressed in college-caps of black velvet with gold tassels, and silk robes of scarlet and white' received their honorary degrees. Cambridge, 'with its peculiar customs which retain much that is medieval, with its colleges that resemble monasteries, and its buildings recalling a remote past' made 'a very agreeable impression' on Tchaikovsky, and he was overwhelmed by the 'extraordinary' hospitality which had been shown to him. He told Jurgenson that he regarded his Cambridge hosts, Professor Maitland and his wife, as 'two of the most charming people' he had ever had the pleasure of meeting.

The day following the ceremony he left for Paris, and wrote to Kondrati:

Now that all is over it is pleasant to look back on my visit to England and to remember the extraordinary cordiality shown to me everywhere, although, in consequence of my peculiar temperament, while there, I tormented and worried myself to fiddle-strings.

Sad news awaited him on his return to Moscow. Both Albrecht and Vladimir Shilovsky had died, and his friend Apukhtin was desperately ill. Modest recalls his brother's uncharacteristic reaction:

A few years earlier, one such grief would have affected Tchaikovsky more deeply than all of them, occurring together, now did. Death now appeared to him less enigmatic and frightening. Whether his feelings were now less acute, or whether the mental sufferings of later years had taught him that death was often a deliverance, I cannot say. I merely lay emphasis on the fact that, despite the discomforting news which greeted him from all directions, from the time of his return from England to the end of his life Tchaikovsky was as serene and cheerful as at any period of his existence.

As soon as he was safely back at Klin, Tchaikovsky resumed work on his sixth symphony. Despite his usual difficulties with orchestration, the score was ready by the end of August and he was able to write triumphantly to Jurgenson:

On my word of honour, I have never felt such self-satisfaction, such pride, such happiness, as in the knowledge that I have created a good thing.

A letter to Bob Davidov, on the other hand, shows that he was much less confident about the reaction of the musical public to his new work:

To me it will seem quite natural, and not in the least astonishing, if this new symphony meets with abuse or scant appreciation at first. I definitely

141

Tchaikovsky photographed
in Cambridge 1893

regard it as quite the best — certainly the most sincere — of all my works. I
love it as I never loved any one of my musical offsprings before.

When news of Apukhtin's death reached him, Tchaikovsky took
it quite calmly, but a letter of this same period (addressed to
Jurgenson) clearly indicates that the von Meck affair still troubled
him: he had been rereading some of her correspondence:

One would think, on reading these letters, that it would be more possible
for fire to turn into water than for her subsidy to cease. One would wonder,

142

rather, how I came to be content with so paltry a sum when she was ready to give me practically all she had. And suddenly — farewell. What is more important — I actually believed that she had lost all her money. But nothing of the kind: simply a woman's fickleness. It is irritating — the devil take it — but I don't give a damn.

After a brief visit to Hamburg, Tchaikovsky took up the first movement of the symphony which he had started the previous autumn, and had subsequently discarded, and re-worked it as the opening movement of a new piano concerto. This single movement was in due course published as the Piano Concerto No. 3 in E flat major, Op 75. Opera, as always, remained uppermost in his mind whenever he was contemplating new projects, and once more he asked his brother, Modest, to find a suitable subject for him. By 19 October 1893, the time had come for him to leave Klin in order to direct rehearsals at St. Petersburg for the first performance of his Symphony No. 6. As the train passed through the village of Frolovskoye, he pointed out the churchyard and remarked to his fellow-passengers, 'I shall be buried there, and people will point out my grave as they go by.' He also mentioned to Taneyev on this occasion that he wished to be buried at Frolovskoye. Neither of these references should be regarded as any kind of premonition of his own imminent death: they were most probably prompted by the fact that he had recently attended the funeral of his friend Zverev in Moscow. Certainly, by the time he reached St. Petersburg on 22 October he was in good health and spirits.

Six days later, Tchaikovsky conducted the new symphony at the opening concert of the season, given by the Russian Musical Society. As he had correctly forecast, the work failed to arouse genuine enthusiasm in the audience and received lukewarm reviews in the press. Only one critic — that of the *Birjevya Viedomosti* — was unreserved in his praise: all the rest echoed the opinion expressed in the *Nvoe Vermya* that 'as far as inspiration is concerned, it stands far below other symphonies'. Throughout his career, as we have seen, Tchaikovsky had always been sensitive, not to say over-sensitive, to hostile criticism in the press and elsewhere. Now, with only a few days to live, he brushed the reviews aside and remained unshaken in his belief that the symphony was 'the best thing I ever composed or ever shall compose'. The morning after the concert, Modest found his brother at the breakfast table in 'excellent spirits', with the score in front of him:

He had agreed to send it to Jurgenson in Moscow that very day, and could not decide upon a title. He did not want to designate it merely by a number, and had abandoned his original intention of calling it 'a programme symphony'. "Why programme," he said, "when I do not intend

A bust of Tchaikovsky, by
an unknown sculptor

to give it?" I suggested 'tragic' as an appropriate title. But this did not please him either. I left the room while Peter Ilyich was still in a state of indecision. Suddenly the word 'pathetic' occurred to me, and I returned to suggest it. I remember as though it were yesterday, how my brother exclaimed: "Bravo', Modest, splendid! *Pathetic*!" Then and there in my presence, he added to the score the title by which the Symphony has always been known.

What Modest does not reveal is that within a matter of hours Tchaikovsky changed his mind and wrote to Jurgenson asking that the title page should bear a simple dedication to Vladimir Lvovich ('Bob') Davidov, the number of the symphony itself and the composer's name — no more. Jurgenson ignored this request, and of course the title *Pathétique* prevailed. It is not surprising that there is no formal programme to the symphony, but a rough draft found among the composer's papers some years after his death perhaps holds the key:

The ultimate essence of the plan of the symphony is LIFE. First part — all impulsive passion, confidence, thirst for activity. Must be short. (Finale DEATH — result of collapse). Second part, love; third, disappointments; fourth ends dying away (also short).

Certainly the music does not suggest a battle with Fate, as in the fourth symphony, but rather an acceptance of the inevitability of life's normal pattern. But there is always a danger in discussing music — even such subjective music as that of Tchaikovsky — in this kind of way: it is for each listener to discover for himself what the symphony contains. And if he finds a mood of pessimism and despair in the music, let him remember that at the time of its composition Tchaikovsky himself was, according to Modest, both 'contented and jovial'. He even managed to joke about death: to an actor-friend he declared:

There is plenty of time before we need reckon with this snub-nosed horror: it will not come to snatch us off just yet! I feel I shall live a long time.

There is further evidence to suggest that, at this time, Tchaikovsky entertained no clear premonition of death, still less that he was contemplating suicide, as has been suggested. In his letter to Jurgenson immediately after the performance of the *Pathétique*, he briefly describes the reaction of the audience, re-affirms his confidence in the work and then adds this revealing sentence.

But we can talk about this soon, for I shall be in Moscow on Saturday.

Hardly the words of a doomed man. And yet what actually followed remains to this day baffling and inexplicable.

*   *   *

Three days after writing the letter to Jurgenson, from which that brief, significant extract has been quoted, Tchaikovsky failed to appear for breakfast and complained to Modest that he had spent a sleepless night suffering from indigestion. He had, in fact, spent the previous evening drinking in a restaurant until two in the morning and it is perhaps not surprising that he assured Modest that his disorder was nothing more serious than his usual 'stomach cramps'. Later, on that same morning of 2 November, he visited Napravnik but felt no better on his return home. Nevertheless, he refused to allow Modest to send for a doctor. At lunch, he was unable to eat, but he joined Modest and Bob Davidov at the table where, to their horror, he drank a glass of unboiled water despite their warnings about the danger of cholera which was, once again, present in the city. He appeared quite unconcerned about risking the dread infection which had carried off his mother. During the afternoon Glazunov called, and found him a very sick man. By the time evening fell, Modest was seriously alarmed and sent for one of the most-reputed physicians in St. Petersburg, Dr. Bertenson. As soon as he saw the condition of his patient, Dr. Bertenson summoned his brother, a fellow-doctor, for a second opinion. Tchaikovsky became weaker and started to complain of severe pains in his chest. He told Modest, 'I believe this is death'.

A third doctor was called and cholera diagnosed. Throughout the night, those around Tchaikovsky's bedside fought to contain the symptoms, and by morning it seemed that their efforts had been rewarded. Tchaikovsky felt better, and claimed to have been 'snatched from the jaws of death'.

But the remission was only temporary. The following day he suffered a relapse and, convinced that death was near, he ordered the doctors to leave. Shortly afterwards he entered the second, more alarming, stage of the disease. His kidneys failed and he became delirious. Alexey Sofronov arrived from Klin, but his master quite failed to recognise him. As a last, desperate remedy, a hot bath treatment was attempted but proved futile. Nikolay sent for a priest to administer the sacrament but, as Modest later recorded, 'his prayers in clear and distinct tones . . . did not seem to reach the ears of the dying man'. Modest also tells us that during his delirium, Tchaikovsky kept repeating the phrase 'accursed one' in an 'indignant or reproachful tone', which he took to be a reference to Madame von Meck. However, the words both for cholera and death itself take the feminine form in the Russian language, and it is just possible that either might have been in Tchaikovsky's mind on his deathbed. At three o'clock on the morning of 6 November 1893, in the presence of his brothers Modest and Nikolay, his beloved nephew Bob Davidov, his loyal servant Alexey Sofronov and the three doctors, an 'indescribable look of clear recognition' passed over his face as Peter Ilyich Tchaikovsky died.

* * *

The real tragedy of Tchaikovsky is that he spent a great part of his life under the shadow of imaginary horrors created by his own sensitive and tortured nature. And just as he was emerging from this shadow, just as he was achieving an emotional balance and maturity, just as he was reaching the height of his creative powers, the imaginary horrors became a reality and Fate, that great Russian obsession, struck him down.

Tchaikovsky's funeral procession in St. Petersburg, 28 October 1893

148

Appendix

The following extracts from three of the letters written to Madame von Meck in 1878 give a fascinating insight into Tchaikovsky's working methods.

To N. F. von Meck.

"Clarens, *March 5th (17th), 1878.*

"It is delightful to talk to you about my own methods of composition. So far I have never had any opportunity of confiding to anyone these hidden utterances of my inner life; partly because very few would be interested, and partly because, of these few, scarcely one would know how to respond to me properly. To you, and you alone, I gladly describe all the details of the creative process, because in you I have found one who has a fine feeling and can understand my music . . .

"You ask me how I manage my instrumentation. I never compose in the *abstract;* that is to say, the musical thought never appears otherwise than in a suitable external form. In this way I invent the musical idea and the instrumentation simultaneously. Thus I thought out the scherzo of our symphony — at the moment of its composition — exactly as you heard it. It is inconceivable except as *pizzicato.* Were it played with the bow, it would lose all its charm and be a mere body without a soul.

"As regards the Russian element in my works, I may tell you that not infrequently I begin a composition with the intention of introducing some folk-melody into it. Sometimes it comes of its own accord, unintentionally (as in the finale of our symphony). As to this national element in my work, its affinity with the folksongs in some of my melodies and harmonies proceeds from my having spent my childhood in the country, and having, from my earliest years, been impregnated with the characteristic beauty of our Russian folk-music. I am passionately fond of the national element in all its varied expressions. In a word, I am Russian in the fullest sense of the word."

To N. F. von Meck.

"Kamenka, *June 24th (July 6th), 1878.*

"You want to know my methods of composing? Do you know, dear friend, that it is very difficult to give a satisfactory answer to your question, because the circumstances under which a new work comes into the world vary considerably in each case.

"First, I must divide my works into two categories, for this is important in trying to explain my methods.

"(1) Works which I compose on my own initiative — that is to say, from an invincible inward impulse.

"(2) Works which are inspired by external circumstances: the wish of a friend, or a publisher, and *commissioned* works.

"Here I should add experience has taught me that the intrinsic value of a work has nothing to do with its place in one or the other of these categories. It frequently happens that a composition which owes its existence to external influences proves very successful; while one that proceeds entirely from my own initiative may, for various indirect reasons, turn out far less well. These indirect circumstances, upon which depends the mood in which a work is written, are of the very greatest importance. During the actual time of creative activity complete quiet is absolutely necessary to the artist. In this sense every work of art, even a musical composition, is *objective.* Those who imagine that a creative artist can — through the medium of his art — express his feelings at the moment when he is *moved,* make the greatest mistake. Emotions — sad or joyful — can only be expressed *retrospectively,* so to speak. Without any special reason for rejoicing, I may be moved by the most cheerful creative mood, and, *vice versâ,* a work composed under the happiest surroundings may be touched with dark and gloomy colour.

The Tchaikovsky monument by Mukhina outside the Moscow Conservatoire

"In a word, an artist lives a double life: an everyday human life, and an artistic life, and the two do not always go hand in hand.

"In any case, it is absolutely necessary for a composer to shake off all the cares of daily existence, at least for a time, and give himself up entirely to his art-life.

"Works belinging to the first category do not require the least effort of will. It is only necessary to obey our inward promptings, and if our material life does not crush our artistic life under its weight of depressing circumstances, the work progresses with inconceivable rapidity. Everything else is forgotten, the soul throbs with an incomprehensible and indescribable excitement, so that, almost before we can follow this swift flight of inspiration, time passes literally unreckoned and unobserved.

"There is something *somnambulistic* about this condition. *On ne s'entend pas vivre.* It is impossible to describe such moments. Everything that flows from one's pen, or merely passes through one's brain (for such moments often come at a time when writing is an impossibility) under these circumstances is *invariably good,* and if no external obstacle comes to hinder the creative glow, the result will be an artist's best and most perfect work. Unfortunately such external hindrances are inevitable. A duty has to be performed, dinner is announced, a letter arrives, and so on. This is the reason why there exist so few compositions which are of equal quality throughout. Hence *the joins, patches, inequalities and discrepancies.*

"For the works in my second category it is necessary to *get into the mood.* To do so we are often obliged to fight with indolence and disinclination. Besides this, there are many other fortuitous circumstances. Sometimes the victory is easily gained. At other times inspiration eludes us, and cannot be recaptured. I consider it, however, the *duty* of an artist not to be conquered by circumstances. He must not wait. Inspiration is a guest who does not care to visit those who are indolent. The reproaches heaped upon the Russian nation because of its deficiency in original works of art are not without foundation, for the Russians are lazy . . .

"I have explained that I compose either from an inward impulse, winged by a lofty and undefinable inspiration, or I simply *work*, invoking all my powers, with sometimes answer and sometimes remain deaf to my invocation. In the latter case the work created will always remain the mere product of labour, without any glow of genuine musical feeling.

"I hope you will not think I am boasting, if I say that my appeal to inspiration is very rarely in vain. In other words, that power which I have already described as a capricious guest has long since become fast friends with me, so that we are inseparable, and it only deserts me when my material existence is beset by untoward circumstances and its presence is of no avail. Under normal conditions I may say there is no hour of the day in which I cannot compose. Sometimes I observe the curiosity that uninterrupted activity, which — independent of the subject of any conversation I may be carrying on — continues its course in that department of my brain which is devoted to music. Sometimes it takes a preparatory form — that is, the consideration of all details that concern the elaboration of some projected work; another time it may be an entirely new and independent musical idea, and I make an effort to hold it fast in my memory. Whence does it come? It is an inscrutable mystery.

"Two o'clock.

"I usually write my sketches on the first piece of paper to hand. I jot them down in the most abbreviated form. A melody never stands alone, but invariably with the harmonies which belong to it. These two elements of music, together with the rhythm, must never be separated; every melodic idea brings its own inevitable harmony and its suitable rhythm. If the harmony is very intricate, I set down in the sketch a few details as to the working out of the parts; when the harmony is quite simple, I only put in the bass, or a figured bass, and sometimes not even this. If the sketch is intended for an orchestral work, the ideas appear ready-coloured by some special instrumental combination. The original plan of instrumentation often undergoes some modifications.

"The text must *never* be written after the music, for if music is written to given words only, those words invoke a suitable musical expression. It is quite possible to fit words to a short melody, but in treating a serious work such adaptation is not permissible. It is equally impossible to compose a symphonic work and afterwards to attach to it a programme, since every episode of the chosen programme should evoke its corresponding musical presentment. This stage of composition — the sketch — is remarkably pleasant and interesting. It brings an indescribable delight, accompanied, however, by a kind of unrest and nervous agitation. Sleep is disturbed and meals forgotten. Nevertheless, the development of the project proceeds tranquilly. The instrumentation of a work which is completely thought out and matured is a most enjoyable task.

"The same does not apply to the bare sketch of a work for pianoforte or voice, or little pieces in general, which are sometimes very tiresome. Just now I am occupied with this kind of work. You ask: do I confine myself to established forms? Yes, and no. Some compositions imply the use of traditional forms; but only as regards their general features — the sequence of the various movements. The details permit of considerable freedom of treatment, if the development of the ideas require it. For example, the first movement of *our* Symphony is written in a very informal style. The second subject, which ought, properly speaking, to be in the major, is in a somewhat remote minor key. In the recapitulation of the principal part the second subject is entirely left out, etc. In the finale, too, there are many deviations from traditional form. In vocal music, in which everything depends on the text, and in fantasias (like *The Tempest* and *Francesca*) the form is quite free. You ask me about melodies built upon the notes of the harmony. I can assure you, and prove it by many examples, that it is quite possible, by means of rhythm and the transposition of these notes, to evolve millions of new and beautiful melodic combinations. But this only applies to homophonic music. With polyphonic music such a method of building up a melody would interfere with the independence of the parts. In the music of Beethoven, Weber, Mendelssohn, Schumann, and especially Wagner, we frequently find melodies which consist of the notes of the common chord; a gifted musician will always be able to invent a new and interesting fanfare. . ."

To N. F. von Meck.

"Kamenka, *June 25th (July 7th), 1878.*

"Yesterday, when I wrote to you about my methods of composing, I did not sufficiently enter into that phase of work which relates to the working out of the sketch. This phase is of primary importance. What has been set down in a moment of ardour must now be critically examined, improved, extended, or condensed, as the form requires. Sometimes one must do oneself violence, must sternly and pitilessly take part against oneself, before one can mercilessly erase things thought out with love and enthusiasm. I cannot complain of poverty of imagination, or lack of inventive power; but, on the other hand, I have always suffered from my want of skill in the management of form. Only after strenuous labour have I at last succeeded in making the form of my compositions correspond, more or less, with their contents. Formerly I was careless and did not give sufficient attention to the critical overhauling of my sketches. Consequently my *seams* showed, and there was no organic union between my individual episodes. This was a very serious defect, and I only improved gradually as time went on; but the form of my works will never be *exemplary*, because, although I can modify, I cannot radically alter the essential qualities of my musical temperament. But I am far from believing that my gifts have yet reached their ultimate development. I can affirm with joy that I make continual progress on the way of self-development, and am passionately desirous of attaining the highest degree of perfection of which my talents are capable. Therefore I expressed myself badly when I told you yesterday that I transcribed my works direct from the first sketches. The process is something more than copying; it is actually a critical examination, leading to corrections, occasional additions, and frequent curtailments. . ."

Tomb of Tchaikovsky

INDEX

Selective listing of references
Illustrations are indicated in bold type

Tchaikovsky: Selective listing of works

Orchestral

156